P9-CAX-478

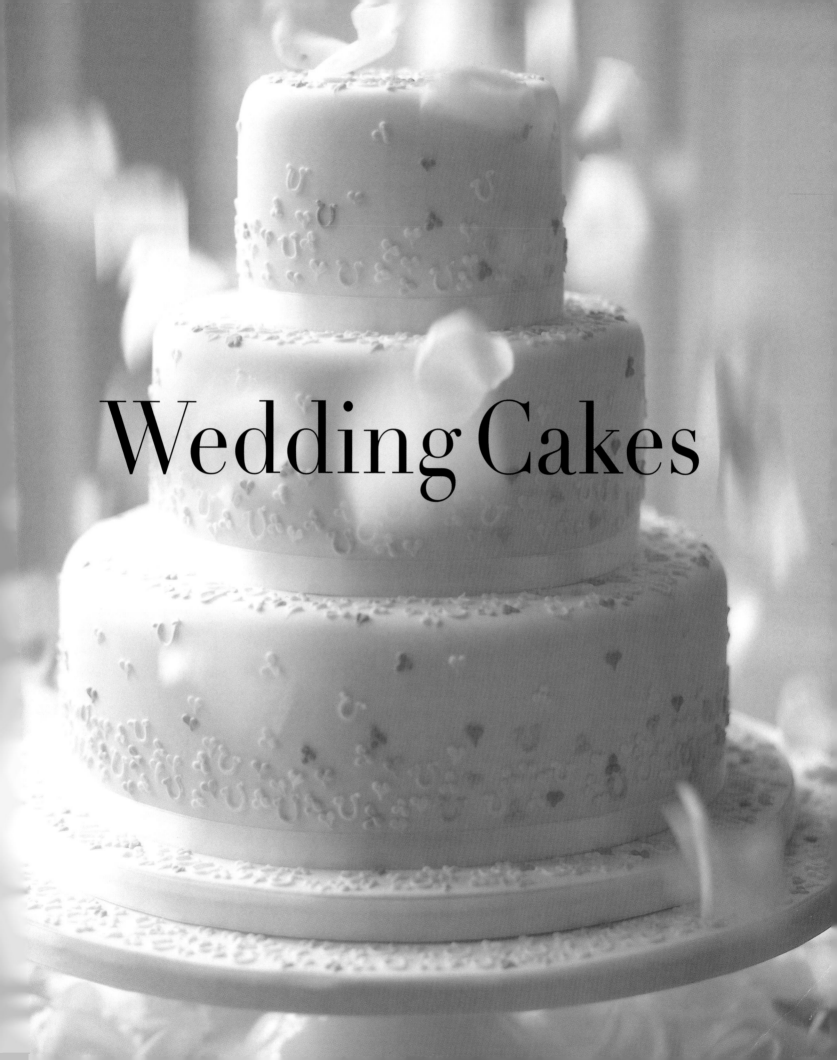

# Wedding Cakes

Mich Turner
*of Little Venice Cake Company*

# Wedding Cakes

photography by
RICHARD JUNG

UNIVERSE

For Phil, Marlow, and
George—my shining stars

First published in the United States of
America in 2009 by Universe Publishing
A Division of Rizzoli International
Publications, Inc.
300 Park Avenue South
New York, NY 10010
www.rizzoliusa.com

Originally published in the United Kingdom
as *Couture Wedding Cakes* in 2009 by
Jacqui Small LLP
An imprint of Aurum Books Ltd
7 Greenland Street
London NW1 0ND

Text copyright © Mich Turner 2009
Photography, design, and layout copyright
© Jacqui Small 2009

All rights reserved. No part of this book
may be reproduced, stored in a retrieval
system, or transmitted in any form or by
any means, electronic, mechanical,
photocopying, recording, or otherwise,
without prior consent of the publishers.

**Publisher** Jacqui Small
**Editorial Manager** Lesley Felce
**Art Director** Maggie Town
**Designer** Beverly Price
**Additional Photography** Janine
Hosegood, Sarah Cuttle
**Editor** Alison Bolus
**Production** Peter Colley

2009 2010 2011 2012 /
10 9 8 7 6 5 4 3 2 1

ISBN 978-0-7893-1814-5

Library of Congress Control Number:
2008932287

Printed in China

# CONTENTS

# FOREWORD

Cake: the word conjures up delicious thoughts.
Put Mich Turner and cake together, and served up
is a sublime mixture of ingredients that provides a
rare glimpse into the world of perfection.

Many strive to be the best, but few achieve it.
Put simply, where cakes are concerned, Mich is
the best, setting standards of excellence at which
we can only marvel.

Mich has honed her talents not just to be the best
in class but to the point where her delicate touch
provides supreme tasting experiences aligned to
presentations that take the breath away.

If this book gives away some of Mich's secrets,
then blessed are we.

Mich is a true British star. Enjoy!

CONRAD FREE
Chairman
Debrett's Limited

# INTRODUCTION

I was privileged and honored to be named the *Harper's Bazaar* and Chanel Entrepreneur of the Year in 2006. One element of my prize was a personal shopping experience with Chanel in London's Old Bond Street. I was afforded the full red-carpet treatment: Champagne on arrival and a personal showcase of the entire collection. I bounced out of the store three hours later with a tailor-made iconic Chanel tweed jacket, a string of pearls, and a bottle of Coco Chanel perfume—and so began my love affair with haute couture.

Since then I have become fascinated by all elements of fashion, using them as sources of inspiration for new wedding cake designs: from the glamorous Tiller Girls at the turn of the twentieth century, and the elegant simplicity of Coco Chanel of the 1930s; through the early days of Karl Lagerfeld and Yves Saint Laurent at the House of Christian Dior in Paris in the 1950s; to modern-day fun and funky Galliano and Christian Lacroix, and the more romantic and contemporary Elie Saab, Matthew Williamson, and Amanda Wakeley.

If the thought of making a wedding cake seems rather daunting, look closely at many of the cakes here and you will see that some are actually quite simple—three tiers stacked or blocked, with minimal decoration—but stunning just the same. A pure white cake with contrasting ribbon trim can be just as eye-catching as a flower-festooned creation. So be inspired: These are all tried-and-tested designs that really do work, and the cake recipes, ranging from traditional fruit and ever-popular sticky date to more unusual lime and coconut, are delicious.

*Mich Turner*

# setting the scene

# THE MAIN ATTRACTION

*Cutting the cake is the first official role of the new bride, and as such it is imperative that the cake is displayed to best effect. The cake should be clearly visible to the guests, provide the perfect setting for a photo opportunity, and be accessible to both the bride and groom and venue waiting staff.*

The idea of the wedding cake dates back to Roman times, when the groom would break a loaf of bread over the bride's head to symbolize prosperity, longevity, and fertility. Later, guests at medieval weddings were known to bring small cakes to a wedding banquet and pile these together on a table to create a stack of cakes over which the bride and groom had to try to kiss each other. This stack of small cakes later evolved into the multitiered wedding cake we have today. An important figure in the development of the tiered wedding cake was a baker named William Rich, who was based in Fleet Street, London, in the nineteenth century. He created a wedding cake for his daughter based on the octagonal steeple of St. Bride's Church in Fleet Street.

The use of a rich fruit cake baked with vine fruits steeped in brandy for a wedding cake came to symbolize wealth, fertility, happiness, longevity, and health, and its keeping properties made it ideal as designs became more complicated and so took longer to decorate. As for the white icing, this was made from costly fine sugar, which meant that only the wealthy could afford to use it. Its use became fashionable after Queen Victoria set the trend of marrying in white. Nowadays the wedding cake—now available in every shade and hue of color, and varying from chic and simple to complex and extravagant—is an important and integral part of the wedding along with the wedding dress and the bride's bouquet.

*"The wedding cake should be center stage at the reception, a star in its own right."*

**opposite** *Venetian presented on a round silver cake stand in front of the marble stone fireplace at the little-known 30 Pavilion Road in Knightsbridge, London. The cake's blocked roses are complemented by tea lights and the bridal bouquet.*

**below** *Queen Elizabeth Diamond on display in the ballroom foyer at Claridge's hotel in London. The five-tier cake, displayed on a bed of yellow-toned flowers, takes center stage, welcoming guests as they enter the ballroom by passing through the revolving doors and up the staircase.*

**WHERE TO PUT THE CAKE** When setting the scene to create the perfect backdrop for the wedding cake, the most important consideration is location. Whether the cake takes center stage in a grand ballroom, is framed by a beautiful fireplace, or is positioned by a sweeping staircase, it is important to think about the ideal time for cutting the cake so it can be presented to best effect within the venue.

The cake should be presented in a prominent position that is easily accessible to the bride and groom and has a pleasing background to ensure a natural photo opportunity. For a more intimate occasion, consider positioning the wedding cake as a centerpiece on the main wedding breakfast table.

Wedding cakes are often presented on the dance floor. While this can create a seemingly perfect space to showcase the cake, caution should be taken if the dance floor is sprung or if the guests will be invited to dance between courses, as this can make the cake unstable. Similarly, wedding cakes may be set up in a marquee, but the ground is rarely level and stable, and for these locations I would advise against a multitiered wedding cake separated with pillars, columns, or flowers— opt instead for a stacked cake, which will be better supported.

*right* Spring Rain set up on the main wedding breakfast table in the Penthouse of The Dorchester hotel in London. The cake is on view for all the guests to admire at this wedding.

*left* Spring Phalaenopsis Orchid presented on a white porcelain stand at the base of a sweeping staircase— a natural spot for the bride and groom to cut the cake.

> *"Use flowers, candles, and lighting to ensure the cake is the star of the reception."*

*opposite* Pearlique is set on a stunningly simple silver-effect cake stand fully dressed with fresh flowers and delicate tea lights.

*right* Amaryllis Pearl is presented on a mirrored Perspex disc dressed with fresh blooms in dramatically contrasting colors to create balance and harmony.

*below* Summer Basket Weave is nestled on a garland of fresh flowers and foliage to lift the wedding cake and carry the theme of the flowers through to the bouquet on top.

Wedding cakes can be displayed on a clothed service trolley, which can be wheeled from the center of the dance floor into the kitchen for cutting, or simply laid on a polished wooden table. Tables do not have to be clothed, but fine linens or sumptuous fabrics can certainly enhance and complement a wedding cake. Damask cloths in shades of ivory add glamour, while colored silks can be more fun and funky. Alternatively, create a topiary tablecloth by studding it with fresh flowers.

**FLOWERS AND CANDLES** Flowers and candles can greatly enhance and complement the table setting for the cake. A silver cake stand can be fully dressed with an abundance of fresh scented flowers; alternatively, stud a polystyrene plinth base with fresh flowers and nestle the wedding cake on top to create a floral garland. Candles should not be positioned too close to the cake, otherwise there is a danger of melting it or singeing the flowers (or even the bride and groom as they cut the cake). Ideally, the cake should be spot-lit from above for maximum effect.

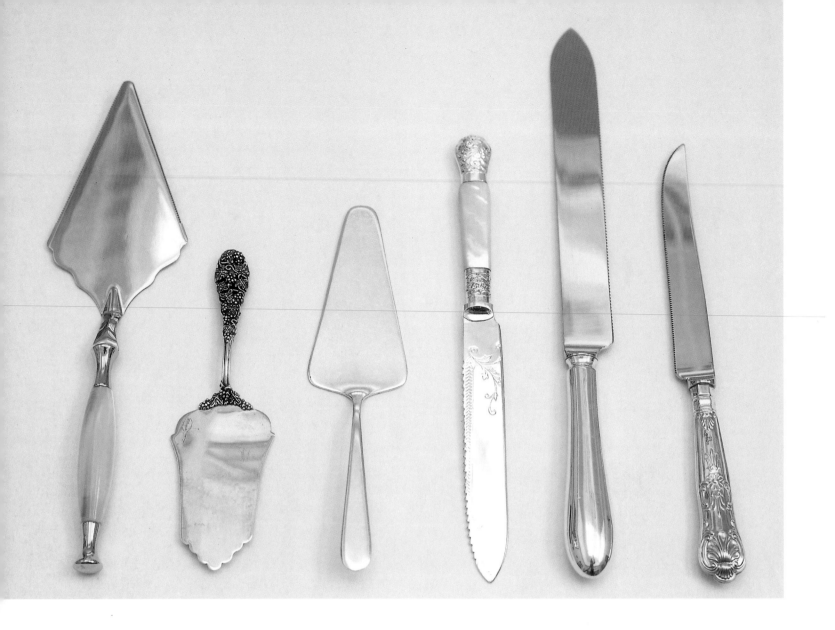

## CAKE STANDS AND KNIVES

The cake on its base board can be set directly onto a table, but there are also a number of options with more dramatic effect. The most popular choice is a polished solid silver square or round cake stand, which can show off a wedding cake simply and elegantly. Beautiful etched glass stands also look stunning, as do solid silver salvers. All of these stands can be used for dinner parties and afternoon teas long after the wedding day is over, so the bride might consider buying a stand rather than hiring it from the wedding venue.

Cube vases filled with flowers, pea lights, or colored water set together as bricks can be a fun method of presenting a cake, while mirrored Perspex discs laid on a polystyrene block of fresh flowers add drama. Monochrome designs, such as Ascot Pearl, would be complemented by black or white china stands.

For a multitiered wedding cake, it is advisable to cut the cake with a proper cake knife, often known as a bride's knife. There are many styles available, including silver, gold, glass-handled, and bone-handled. If the knife is bought rather than hired, it could be engraved with the names of the bride and groom and the date of the wedding. It can then be kept and passed down through the family as a cherished heirloom. Another choice is to use a dramatic silver sword, such as a reproduction Scottish claymore, which could also be engraved to commemorate the day.

An ornate cake slicer would be more appropriate if the wedding cake will be served as a dessert.

Traditionally, the bride and groom are invited to cut the cake after the formal speeches have been made at the end of the wedding reception.

*opposite* A collection of cake knives and servers in a variety of sizes and styles, both plain and decorative, and some with contrasting handles for interest.

*right* A selection of cake stands, clockwise from top right: round solid silver cake stand with Little Venice Lace; etched glass cake stand with Vintage Rose Crown; solid silver shell and scroll salver with Sea Pearls; white porcelain cake stand with Parisian Pearl; square silver-effect cake stand with Bows and Brooches; black lacquered cake stand with Ascot Pearl.

## CUTTING THE CAKE

The bride puts her right hand on the knife, then the groom puts his hand on top of hers with his other arm around her waist. The bride then grasps the knife gently with her left hand, so showing off her ring.

With a tiered cake, it is always the base tier that is cut and served; the bride and groom can then cut small tasters from it. With stands of individual cakes, there may be a larger top tier to cut. Rather than attempt to cut all the way through this tier, which could make the stand unstable, the couple should just pose with the knife, then cut taster pieces from one of the small cakes with a pastry fork to give to each other.

For a less formal celebration or Champagne reception, it can be appropriate to set the cake table with Champagne glasses and linen napkins. The bride and groom can make a Champagne toast by the cake and seal it with a kiss.

*above* A decorated Autumnal Candy Stripe individually presented with a Champagne tea. The classic, low-key tableware provides the perfect setting for these elaborate little cakes.

*right* A generous slice of wedding cake served on a highly decorative plate with a pastry fork for ease of eating. The cake can be accompanied by a cup of tea and glass of chilled Champagne.

*opposite* The bride and groom cutting the base tier of the wedding cake. It is traditional for the bride and groom to feed each other a mouthful of the cake.

glamorous

# QUEEN ELIZABETH DIAMOND

*I designed this cake to celebrate the Diamond Wedding anniversary of HRH Queen Elizabeth II and Prince Philip in 2007. The pearl design is repeated six times around each tier, one for each decade of marriage. The tiers are separated by columns of white sugar roses and leaves, studded with Swarovski crystals.*

## YOU WILL NEED

8-inch, 12-inch, and 16-inch round cakes

two 8-inch, 12-inch, and 16-inch thin round cake boards

8-inch, 12-inch, and 16-inch round polystyrene dummies 3 inches deep, for the tiers

19 lb. marzipan, for the cakes

47 lb. 8 oz. rolled fondant—26 lb. 7 oz. for the cakes, 9 lb. 8 oz. for the boards, 5 lb. for the columns, and 6 lb. 9 oz. for the roses and leaves

11-inch, 15-inch, 20-inch, and 22-inch thick round cake boards

2 quantities royal icing (see page 133)

6¼ yards ivory ribbon ⅝ inch wide, cut into 36-inch, 48-inch, 63-inch, and 69-inch lengths

glue stick

6-inch and 10-inch round polystyrene dummies 5 inches deep, for the columns

6-inch and 10-inch thin round cake boards, for the columns

sharp knife

waxed paper and pen

scribe

¾-inch rose-leaf plunger veiner and cutter

5 pastry bags

nos. 1.5, 2, 3, and 4 tips

4 tsp. topaz luster

3 tbsp. edible gel

paintbrush

3¼ yards ivory ribbon 1 inch wide, cut into 26-inch, 39-inch, and 52-inch lengths

sharp scissors

20 white 28-gauge wires, cut into 3

60 Swarovski ⅜-inch bicone crystal beads

16 doweling rods

**1** Place the 8-inch cake on a thin board, then on a shallow polystyrene dummy, and then on a second thin board, all of the same size. Repeat using the 12-inch and 16-inch cakes, thin boards, and dummies. Cover each column with a layer of marzipan (3 lb., 6 lb., and 10 lb. respectively) and rolled fondant (4 lb. 12 oz., 8 lb. 7 oz., and 13 lb. 4 oz. respectively), following the techniques on pages 128 and 130–1. Cover the thick cake boards (the baseboards) with rolled fondant (see pages 130–1 for quantities and technique); let firm overnight.

**2** Put a dab of royal icing on the largest baseboard and place the other baseboard centrally on top. Position the bottom tier centrally on the stacked boards, again using icing. Attach the other 2 tiers to the 2 remaining boards. Fix a length of ⅝-inch ribbon around all 4 boards using a glue stick.

**3** Fix the deep polystyrene dummies onto thin cake boards of the same size with icing. Roll 1 lb. 10 oz. rolled fondant into a piece roughly 5 x 20 inches for the 6-inch dummy and 3 lb. 4 oz. rolled fondant into a piece roughly 5 x 32 inches for the 10-inch dummy. Wet the dummies and roll over the fondant to fix; trim and let firm.

**4** Trace the designs from the templates on pages 153, 156, and 157 and scribe them onto the relevant tiers 6 times. Make 140 hand-molded roses, following the technique on page 136, and 60 rose leaves of varying sizes (1½ inches, 2 inches, and 2½ inches) using the leaf cutter and veiner, following the technique on page 110.

**5** Fit 4 of the pastry bags with the tips and fill with royal icing. Begin with no. 4 for the main pearl drops and diamanté drops. Then use no. 3 for the pearls above this line, no. 2 for the larger pearls and drops inside each star, and no. 1.5 for the smallest pearls and the outline of each star; let set 4 hours or overnight.

**6** Blend the topaz luster with half the edible gel to form a paste. Brush the main piped pearl detail with this glaze and use clear edible gel alone to glaze the stars. Wrap a length of 1-inch ribbon around the base of each tier, trim neatly, and fix with a dab of icing.

**7** Fill the remaining pastry bag with icing and snip the end off. Use the icing to fix the roses and leaves in position around the columns, being careful not to go up over the top (place a larger plain cake board on top of the column as a guide).

**8** Push a wire length through each of the crystals until the crystal is halfway along the wire. Bend the wire over so that the 2 halves meet under the crystal, and twist to secure. Push the wired crystals between the roses into the iced columns; let set.

**9** Dowel the base and middle tiers, following the technique on page 143. Stack the cakes and columns, icing the columns to the cakes above and below for stability.

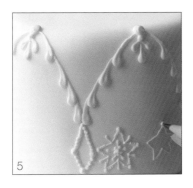

## LENGTHS OF RIBBON REQUIRED (APPROX.)

| Size of round tier cake | 8 inches | 12 inches | 16 inches | |
|---|---|---|---|---|
| Length of ribbon | 26 inches | 39 inches | 52 inches | |
| Size of round board | 11 inches | 15 inches | 20 inches | 22 inches |
| Length of ribbon | 36 inches | 48 inches | 63 inches | 69 inches |

## QUANTITIES OF MARZIPAN AND ROLLED FONDANT REQUIRED

| Size of cake | 8 inches | 12 inches | 16 inches |
|---|---|---|---|
| Quantity of marzipan | 3 lb. | 6 lb. | 10 lb. |
| Quantity of rolled fondant | 4 lb. 13 oz. | 8 lb. 6 oz. | 13 lb. |
| Size of column | 6 inches | 10 inches | |
| Quantity of marzipan | – | – | |
| Quantity of rolled fondant | 1 lb. 10 o.z | 3 lb. 5oz. | |

# LITTLE VENICE LACE™

*This is our iconic Little Venice Cake Company design, which was inspired by luxurious silk and velvet flocking. I featured a single, heart-shaped cake of this design for intimate weddings in my previous book, Party Cakes, but for a wedding cake with more impact and breathtaking beauty, try four tiers!*

## YOU WILL NEED

6-inch, 9-inch, 12-inch, and 15-inch round cakes

6-inch, 9-inch, 12-inch, and 15-inch thin round cake boards

marzipan, for the cakes
(see page 129 for quantities)

ivory rolled fondant, for the cakes and boards
(see pages 130 and 131 for quantities)

9-inch, 12-inch, 15-inch, and 18-inch thick round cake boards

5 yards ivory ribbon ⅝ inch wide, cut into 30-inch, 39-inch, 48-inch, and 57-inch lengths

glue stick

waxed paper and pen

scribe

pastry bag

no. 2 tip

1½ quantities royal icing (see page 133), colored with concentrated ivory edible food color

4 yards ivory ribbon ½ inch wide, cut into 20-inch, 30-inch, 39-inch, and 48-inch lengths

sharp scissors

4-inch, 7-inch, and 10-inch polystyrene columns 2 inches deep

12 doweling rods

27 floral wires, cut into 3

3 heads of white hydrangea and 80 Bianca roses

**1** Place the cakes on thin cake boards of the same size and cover with marzipan and ivory rolled fondant, following the techniques on pages 128 and 130–1. Cover the thick cake boards (the baseboards) with rolled fondant, following the technique on page 130. Fix a length of ⅝-inch ribbon around the edge of each baseboard using a glue stick; let firm overnight. Place each cake on its baseboard. Trace the design from the template on page 154 and scribe it onto each tier of the cake.

**2** Fit the pastry bag with the tip and fill with ivory royal icing. Pipe the design onto the cake. Wrap a length of ½-inch ribbon around the base of each tier, trim neatly, and hold in position with a dab of icing.

**3** Block the tiers with the flowers, following the technique on page 140. Dress the top tier to finish.

# VENETIAN

*I particularly like this sophisticated combination of ivory, caramel, and taupe. The design was inspired by traditional Venetian glass etchings on gorgeous stemware. The combination of the detailed icing and sumptuous roses creates a cake that is quite regal and suitable for a more formal wedding celebration.*

## YOU WILL NEED

6-inch, 8-inch, and 10-inch round cakes

6-inch, 8-inch, and 10-inch thin round cake boards

marzipan, for the cakes (see page 129 for quantities)

ivory rolled fondant, for the cakes and boards (see pages 130 and 131 for quantities)

9-inch, 11-inch, and 13-inch thick round cake boards

3¼ yards caramel ribbon ⅝ inch wide, cut into 30-inch, 36-inch, and 44-inch lengths

glue stick

waxed paper and pen

scribe

2 pastry bags

nos. 1.5 and 2 tips

1 quantity royal icing (see page 133) colored with concentrated taupe edible food color

2¼ yards caramel ribbon ½ inch wide, cut into 20-inch, 26-inch, and 32-inch lengths

sharp scissors

4-inch and 6-inch polystyrene columns 2 inches deep

8 doweling rods

14 Metallica roses and 14 Vandella roses, for the tiers, plus extra for the top

12 floral wires, cut into 3

3 yards dark brown ribbon ⅝ inch wide, cut into 8-inch lengths

**1** Place the cakes on thin cake boards of the same size and cover with marzipan and ivory rolled fondant, following the techniques on pages 128 and 130–1. Cover the thick cake boards (the baseboards) with ivory rolled fondant, following the technique on page 130. Fix lengths of ⅝-inch caramel ribbon around the baseboards using a glue stick; let firm overnight.

**2** Trace the design from the template on pages 152–3 and scribe it onto each tier of the cake.

**3** Fit the pastry bags with the tips and fill with taupe royal icing. Use no. 2 to pipe the hearts and larger pearls of the design and no.1.5 to fill in all the smaller pearls and the leaf garlands. Wrap a length of ½-inch caramel ribbon around the base of each tier, trim neatly, and hold in position with a dab of royal icing.

**4** Block the tiers with the flowers, following the technique on page 140. Tie the lengths of ⅝-inch brown ribbon around half of the roses (close to the calyx) and trim the ribbon ends to points with sharp scissors. When fixing the roses into the columns, intersperse the beribboned and plain roses, so the ribbons peep out between the flowers. Dress the top tier to finish.

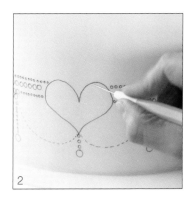

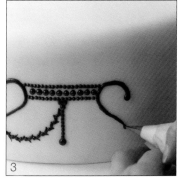

# AMARYLLIS PEARL

*The refined opulence of the Art Deco era was the inspiration for this cake, with its combination of jet black, pure white, and regal purple. The tiers are of different depths and are presented on a mirrored plate set on a bed of fresh flowers, including some stunning Mont Blanc amaryllis blooms.*

## YOU WILL NEED

6-inch and 10-inch round cakes, and a half-depth 8-inch round cake

6-inch, 10-inch, and 13-inch thin round cake boards, plus a 6-inch thin board to scribe around

8-inch thick round cake board

marzipan, to cover the cakes (see page 129 for quantities)

rolled fondant, to cover the cakes and baseboard (see pages 130 and 131 for quantities)

3 yards purple ribbon ⅝ inch wide

sharp scissors

1 quantity royal icing (see page 133), divided into 3 and colored with concentrated edible food colors as follows: ⅓ purple, ⅓ black, and ⅓ left white

4-inch round polystyrene column 2 inches deep

glue stick

10 doweling rods

16-inch round mirrored Perspex disc or plate

scribe

4 pastry bags

1 no. 1.5, 2 no. 2, and 1 no. 3 tips

deep violet hellebores, purple anemones, Mont Blanc amaryllis, Hot Chocolat calla lilies, viburnum berries, and galax leaves

**1** Place the 6-inch and 10-inch cakes on thin boards of the same size and place the half-depth 8-inch cake on a thick board of the same size. Cover with marzipan and rolled fondant, following the techniques on pages 128 and 130–1. Cover the 13-inch thin board (the baseboard) with rolled fondant, following the technique on page 130; let firm overnight.

**2** Wrap 26 inches of the ribbon around the base of the second tier, trim neatly, and hold in position with a dab of royal icing. Wrap the remaining ribbon around the polystyrene column and fix with a glue stick. Stack the top 2 tiers centrally, following the technique on page 141. Fix the base tier to the covered board using a dab of icing. Fix the baseboard and tier centrally on the mirrored disc with icing. Place the 6-inch thin board centrally on top of the base tier and scribe around it; remove the board.

**3** Fit 4 pastry bags with tips and fill with icing as follows: no. 1.5 with purple; no. 2 with white; no. 2 with black; and no. 3 with white. Starting on the top of the base tier, pipe a ring of black pearls around the scribed line. Pipe a row of white pearls with the no. 2 tip from every other black pearl and shorter rows of purple pearls in between, either doing all one color then the other, or changing color as you work around the cake.

**4** Pipe rows of white pearls around the base of the base tier with the no. 3 tip.

**5** Take the purple pearls down onto the board and mirrored disc. Pipe rows of pearls around the join between the top and middle tiers; let dry.

**6** Dowel the base tier following the technique on page 143. Position the central column and place the top 2 tiers in position. Dress with the fresh flowers.

## TIP

This cake has been displayed on a bed of fresh flowers, using a plinth of polystyrene for support. This accentuates a smaller cake while carrying the decorative theme through.

## SEA PEARLS
*Nautical influences have always featured in couture and fashion, with shells, scales, and mermaid-tail gowns constantly being reinvented and showcasing on the catwalk. This Sea Pearls design features clusters of white glazed pearls for a simple, yet stunning, design, topped with fresh orchids.*

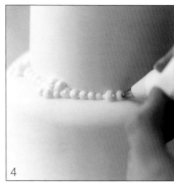

### YOU WILL NEED

4-inch, 6-inch, 8-inch, and 10-inch round cakes

4-inch, 6-inch, 8-inch, 10-inch, and 14-inch thick round cake boards

marzipan, for the cakes
(see page 129 for quantities)

rolled fondant, for the cakes and board
(see pages 130 and 131 for quantities)

18 doweling rods

1¼ yards ivory ribbon ⅝ inch wide

glue stick

scribe

ruler

pastry bag

no. 3 tip

1 quantity royal icing (see page 133)

4 tsp. edible gel

paintbrush

3 *Phalaenopsis* orchids

**1** Place the cakes on thick cake boards of the same size and cover with marzipan and white rolled fondant, following the techniques on pages 128 and 130–1. Cover the 14-inch cake board (the baseboard) with rolled fondant, following the technique on page 130; let firm overnight.

**2** Stack the tiers centrally, following the technique on page 141, and fix the ribbon around the baseboard using a glue stick.

**3** Use the scribe to mark out 8 points around the base of the top tier. This can be done by eye, looking down onto the cake from above. Mark north, south, east, and west points, then the mid points in between. Use a ruler to continue these points vertically down over the other tiers, marking the same points on the cake board at the base of each cake.

**4** Fit the pastry bag with the tip and fill with royal icing. Starting at the base of the top tier, pipe a cluster of large pearls directly over one of the scribed points. Make a line of pearls along to the next marked point, descending in size as you go. When you reach the next mark, make another cluster of pearls. Repeat around the entire tier, then with the other tiers, working downward; let firm.

**5** Paint edible gel on the pearls using a paintbrush to create a sparkling, sea-washed effect. Dress the cake with 3 simple *Phalaenopsis* orchids.

## YOU WILL NEED

4-inch, 6-inch, 8-inch, and 10-inch round cakes

4-inch, 6-inch, 8-inch, 10-inch, and 13-inch thick round cake boards

marzipan, for the cakes (see page 129 for quantities)

rolled fondant, for the cakes and baseboard (see pages 130 and 131 for quantities)

3¼ yards white double satin ribbon 1⅜ inches wide, cut into 14-inch and 26-inch lengths; the rest for the bows

sharp scissors

1 quantity royal icing (see page 133)

4 yards white grosgrain ribbon ⅝ inch wide, cut into 14-inch, 20-inch, 26-inch, 32-inch, and 44-inch lengths

18 doweling rods

glue stick

pastry bag

no 1.5 tip

white silk rose

# PARISIAN PEARL
*Sexy and chic, my Parisian Pearl was inspired by Coco Chanel and Marlene Dietrich, with their elegant black and white couture and sophisticated cigarette holders. By using a contrasting color ribbon behind the narrow one and for the bows (see page 34), you can personalize this design to suit any wedding.*

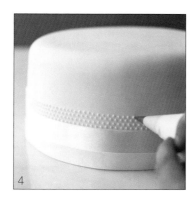

**1** Place the cakes on thick cake boards of the same size and cover with marzipan and rolled fondant, following the techniques on pages 128 and 130–1. Cover the largest board (the baseboard) with rolled fondant, following the technique on page 130; let firm overnight.

**2** Wrap a length of 1⅜-inch ribbon around the base of the top and third tiers, trim neatly, and hold in position with a dab of royal icing. Overlay this with lengths of ⅝-inch grosgrain ribbon. On the second and base tiers, use just the ⅝-inch grosgrain ribbon.

**3** Stack the tiers centrally, following the technique on page 141, and fix into position on the baseboard with a little royal icing. Fix the remaining length of ⅝-inch ribbon around the edge of the baseboard using a glue stick. Use the remaining 2⅛ yards of the 1⅜-inch ribbon to make 2 bows; set aside.

**4** Fit the pastry bag with the tip and fill with royal icing. Starting with the top tier, pipe a single row of delicate pearls just above the double satin ribbon, spaced roughly ⅛ inch apart. Pipe the next row above and in between the first. Repeat up the side of the tier, finishing with a neat row around the top flush with the top of the tier. Repeat with the other tiers, working downward; let set overnight. Ice the 2 ribbon bows in place and put the silk rose on top.

# CORSETIÈRE

*I was inspired by glamorous bronze silk corsets with black lace detailing for this cake. Beautifully structured corsets can be worn in their own right (think John Paul Gaultier!) or provide the perfect shape for tailored clothes. The chocolate tiers are lustered with bronze before the intricate black pearl design is added. (See main picture on page 35.)*

## YOU WILL NEED

4-inch, 6-inch, 8-inch, and 10-inch round cakes

4-inch, 6-inch, 8-inch, 10-inch, and 13-inch thick round cake boards

marzipan or white chocolate plastique (see page 135), for the cakes (see page 129 for quantities)

chocolate rolled fondant, for the cakes (see page 130 for quantities)

2 tbsp. plus 2 tsp. bronze luster

edible varnish spray (optional)

black rolled fondant, for the baseboard (see page 131 for quantity)

glue stick

44 inches black double satin ribbon ⅝ inch wide

waxed paper and pen

scribe

2 pastry bags

nos. 1.5 and 2 tips

1 quantity royal icing (see page 133), colored with concentrated black edible food color

2¾ yards black double satin ribbon ½ inch wide, cut into 14-inch, 20-inch, 26-inch, and 32-inch lengths

sharp scissors

18 doweling rods

silk rose

**1** Place the cakes on thick cake boards of the same size and cover with marzipan or white chocolate plastique, topped with chocolate rolled fondant, following the techniques on pages 128 and 130–1.

**2** Using your fingers, rub bronze luster over all the cakes until they are fully lustered. If you are using the edible varnish, which will add shine to the lustered cake and help the royal iced pearls to adhere, spray the cakes now.

**3** Cover the largest cake board (the baseboard) with black rolled fondant, following the technique on page 130. Use a glue stick to attach the black ribbon around the side of the baseboard. Let the cakes and board firm overnight.

**4** Trace enough of the template on page 155 to fit around the base tier. Use the scribe to prick the design through onto the base tier. Reuse the template for the other tiers, working upward and cutting off the excess paper each time. Omit the middle line of pearls on the top and third tiers, as shown on page 35.

**5** Fit the pastry bags with the tips, and fill both bags with black royal icing. Wrap a length of black ribbon around the base of each tier, trim neatly, and hold in position with a dab of icing.

**6** Pipe the pearl design over the scribed marks, using the no. 2 tip for the larger pearls and the no. 1.5 tip for the more detailed scalloped design; let firm overnight. Stack the tiers centrally, following the technique on page 141, and dress the top tier with the silk rose.

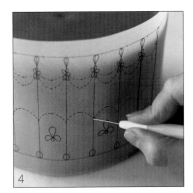
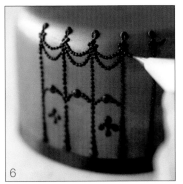

# ASCOT PEARL

*Ladies' Day at Royal Ascot is undoubtedly the world's most glamorous race day, when sensational attire and millinery are traditionally worn. This cake was inspired by the black and white Ascot scene in the movie* My Fair Lady, *starring Audrey Hepburn, whose preferred designer was Hubert de Givenchy.*

## YOU WILL NEED

6-inch, 9-inch, and 12-inch round cakes

6-inch, 9-inch, 12-inch, and 15-inch thick round cake boards

marzipan, for the cakes (see page 129 for quantities)

ivory rolled fondant, for the cakes (see page 130 for quantities)

black rolled fondant, for the baseboard (see page 131 for quantity)

2½ yards black ribbon with white polka dots 1 inch wide, cut into 20-inch, 30-inch, and 39-inch lengths

sharp scissors

1 quantity royal icing (see page 133), colored with concentrated black edible food color

12 doweling rods

glue stick

4 feet black ribbon ⅜ inch wide

pastry bag

no. 2 tip

3½ oz. black gum paste

11 white 26-gauge wires, cut into 3

confectioners' sugar, for dusting

small rolling pin

2-inch camellia cutter

white floral tape

**1** Place the cakes on thick cake boards of the same size and cover with marzipan and ivory rolled fondant, following the techniques on pages 128 and 130–1. Cover the largest cake board (the baseboard) with black rolled fondant, following the technique on page 130; let firm overnight.

**2** Wrap a length of polka-dot ribbon around the base of each tier, trim neatly, and hold in position with a dab of royal icing. Stack the tiers centrally, following the techniqe on page 141. Use a glue stick to attach the black ribbon around the edge of the baseboard.

**3** Fit the pastry bag with the tip and fill with black royal icing. Pipe a row of black pearls above each ribbon.

**4** To make the camellia, knead the black gum paste until smooth and pliable. Mold a hazelnut-sized piece of gum paste into a square-based cone, ⅛ inch wide x ¾ inch long, and insert a wire at the base.

**5** On a clean countertop lightly dusted with confectioners' sugar, roll out the remaining paste to a depth of ⅛ inch. Cut out 10 camellia petals, using the cutter, and insert a wire in the base of each. Drape over a cardboard tube covered with plastic wrap to firm overnight.

**6** To assemble the camellia, wire 4 petals equidistantly around the central cone, using the white floral tape to hold them in position as you work.

**7** Wire the remaining 6 petals equidistantly behind the first row. Trim the wires at the back of the camellia and set in position.

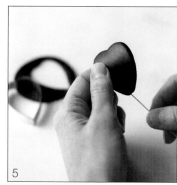

# PEARL FEATHERS

*This cake was inspired by the Tiller Girls dancing troupe from the turn of the twentieth century, with their glittering costumes of sequins and pearls and ostrich plumes. Delicate white feathers are painted onto a pearl-lustered steel-blue cake, then defined with white pearls. A single orchid provides a feathery "headdress."*

## YOU WILL NEED

4-inch, 6-inch, 8-inch, and 10-inch round cakes

4-inch, 6-inch, 8-inch, and 10-inch thick round cake boards

marzipan, for the cakes (see page 129 for quantities)

steel-blue rolled fondant, for the cakes (see page 130 for quantities)

4 tsp. pearl luster

18 doweling rods

scribe

1 tsp. cocoa butter

½ tsp. white powder dust

small paintbrush

2¾ yards white ribbon ⅜ inch wide, cut into 14-inch, 20-inch, 26-inch, and 32-inch lengths

sharp scissors

1 quantity royal icing (see page 133)

pastry bag

no. 2 tip

*Cattleya* orchid

**1** Place the cakes on thick cake boards of the same size and cover with marzipan and steel-blue rolled fondant, following the techniques on pages 128 and 130–1. Using your hands, gently rub pearl luster over each tier; let firm overnight.

**2** Stack the tiers centrally, following the technique on page 141. Use the scribe to mark out the layout of the feathers down over the sides of the entire cake.

**3** Melt the cocoa butter by placing it on a saucer over a bowl of freshly boiled water. Add the white powder dust and blend together, then paint the feathers on the cake with this mixture, building up layers and intensity as you work; let dry. Wrap a length of ribbon around the base of each tier, trim neatly, and hold in position with a dab of royal icing.

**4** Fit the pastry bag with the tip and fill with royal icing. Pipe little pearls over all the main veins of the feathers; let set overnight. Finally, place the orchid on top.

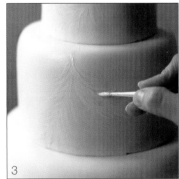

# BOWS AND BROOCHES
*This timeless and classic cake was inspired by sleek couture bridal gowns with soft pearl-luster sashes and a detailed bow. You can easily adapt it to suit any wedding theme simply by changing the color of the icing "ribbons." With no floral or other embellishments, all the elements of this elegantly simple cake are edible.*

## YOU WILL NEED

4-inch, 6-inch, 8-inch, and 10-inch square cakes

4-inch, 6-inch, 8-inch, 10-inch, and 12-inch thick square cake boards

marzipan, for the cakes
(see page 129 for quantities)

rolled fondant, for the cakes and baseboard
(see pages 130 and 131 for quantities),
plus 3 lb. 5 oz. for the ribbons, bow, and brooch

18 doweling rods

glue stick

5 feet ivory ribbon ⅝ inch wide

confectioners' sugar, for dusting

rolling pin

ruler

sharp knife

flat paintbrush

2-inch and 3-inch round cutters

pastry bag

no. 1.5 tip

1 quantity royal icing (see page 133)

45 ¼-inch silver dragees

1 tsp. topaz luster

2 tsp. alcohol dipping solution

**1** Place the cakes on thick cake boards of the same size and cover with marzipan and rolled fondant, following the techniques on pages 128 and 130–1. Cover the largest cake board (the baseboard) with rolled fondant, following the technique on page 130; let firm overnight.

**2** Stack the tiers centrally, following the technique on page 141. Use a glue stick to attach the ivory ribbon around the side of the baseboard.

**3** On a clean countertop lightly dusted with confectioners' sugar, knead the rolled fondant for the ribbons, bow, and brooch until soft and pliable; divide into 3. Form one-third into a sausage shape and roll until it is about 39 inches long and ⅛ inch thick. Place a ruler gently on the icing and cut along the 2 long edges with a sharp knife; slide the ruler along and cut again, repeating until you have cut a 39-inch ribbon of the width of the ruler.

**4** Paint around the bottom of the base tier with a little cooled boiled water and carefully wrap the icing ribbon around it, insuring the base touches the board. Use the knife to trim any excess and join the clean edges together neatly.

**5** Roll out another one-third of the fondant, adding in the trimmings from the first ribbon, and use it to make ribbons for the other 3 tiers, and also the tails, one 6 inches long and one 7 inches long. Attach the ribbons as before and set the tails aside.

**6** To make the bow, roll out a 3-inch ball of rolled fondant to a depth of ⅛ inch and cut out two 3-inch circles. Run a rolling pin over these circles to elongate them slightly, then fold them in half to form 2 loops, joining the shortest sections together. Seal with a little water and set aside.

**7** To make the brooch, roll out the remaining rolled fondant to a depth of ¼ inch and cut out a 2-inch circle. Fit the pastry bag with the tip and fill with royal icing. Pipe 2 rings of pearls around the outer edge of the brooch and fix the silver dragees into position.

**8** Fill in the center of the brooch with more pearls. Using some royal icing, fix the 2 ribbon tails and the 2 bow loops into position on the second tier. Hold the bow in position with toothpicks; let firm 4 hours or overnight.

**9** Dissolve the topaz luster in the alcohol dipping solution and brush 2 coats onto all the iced ribbons, the bow, and its tails, ensuring all the sides and edges are evenly covered. Luster the center of the brooch and finally fix it into position with some royal icing.

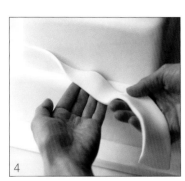

# CASCADING CRYSTAL ROSE

*These roses and lilies cascade down over one side of the cake in much the same way as a luxurious Grecian-style evening gown with a single shoulder strap of corsage blooms by Ben de Lisi. Swarovski crystals dotted among the flowers add sparkle and even more glamour.*

## YOU WILL NEED

6-inch, 8-inch, and 10-inch round cakes

6-inch, 8-inch, 10-inch, 13-inch, and 16-inch thick round cake boards

marzipan, for the cakes (see page 129 for quantities)

rolled fondant, for the cakes (see page 130 for quantities), plus 10½ oz. for the roses

black rolled fondant, for the baseboards (see page 131 for quantities)

5 yards black double satin ribbon ⅜ inch wide, cut into 44-inch and 52-inch lengths for the baseboards and 20-inch, 26-inch, and 32-inch lengths for the cakes

glue stick

1 quantity royal icing (see page 133), colored with concentrated black edible food color, for the pearls, plus extra white icing to fix the flowers

12 doweling rods

scribe

ruler

sharp scissors

2¼ yards silver ribbon ⅜ inch wide, cut into 20-inch, 26-inch, and 32-inch lengths

pastry bag

no. 3 tip

150 silver dragees

12 white sugar lilies (see page 144)

5 white 28-gauge wires, cut into 3

15 Swarovski ⅜-inch bicone crystal beads

**1** Place the cakes on thick cake boards of the same size and cover with marzipan and rolled fondant, following the techniques on pages 128 and 130–1. Cover the 2 largest boards (the baseboards) with black rolled fondant, following the technique on page 130. Make 15 hand-molded roses, following the technique on page 136; let firm overnight.

**2** Fix black ribbon around the edge of the baseboards using a glue stick. Stack the boards together, using icing to fix them. Stack the tiers centrally, following the technique on page 141 and place on the stacked boards.

**3** Scribe a line around the base of each tier using a ruler width as a gauge. Wrap black ribbon around the base of each tier, trim neatly, and hold in place with a dab of royal icing. Repeat with silver ribbon, aligned at each tier base.

**4** Fit the pastry bag with the tip and fill with black royal icing. Pipe a row of black pearl drops around each tier, finishing at the scribed line.

**5** Pipe a single pearl at the top of each pearl drop and place a silver dragee in position; let set. Fix a cascade of roses and lilies from the top tier down over one side of the cake with white icing. Push a wire length through one of the crystals until the crystal is halfway along the wire. Bend the wire over so that the halves meet under the crystal and twist to secure. Repeat with the other crystals and wires. Push the Swarovski crystals in between the roses and the lilies to finish.

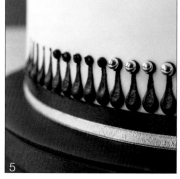

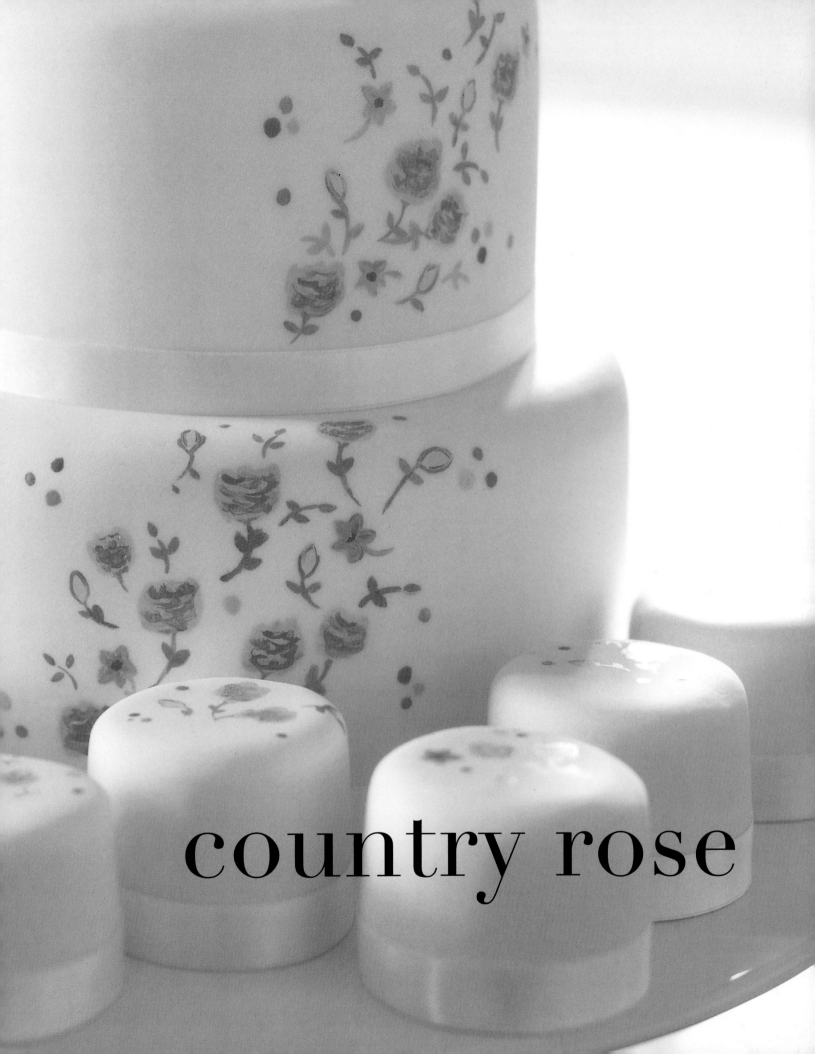

country rose

# ANTIQUE ROSE

*This cake uses the more traditional royal icing, rather than rolled fondant. It is decorated with piped scrolls and pearls, finished with tiny handmade rosebuds, and blocked with fresh flowers. It is formal yet romantic and elegant, dressed with muted colors of dusky pink, lime green, and antique ivory.*

### YOU WILL NEED

6-inch, 9-inch, and 12-inch square cakes

9-inch, 12-inch, and 15-inch thick square cake boards

marzipan, for the cakes
(see page 129 for quantities)

royal icing (see page 133), colored with concentrated ivory edible food color, for the cakes (see page 134 for quantities), plus 10½ oz. for the boards and 1 quantity for the piping

3½ oz. dusky pink gum paste

3½ oz. lime green gum paste

confectioners' sugar, for dusting

small rolling pin

small knife

waxed paper and pen

scribe

pastry bag

no. 2 tip

4 yards ivory ribbon ⅝ inch wide, cut into 36-inch, 48-inch, and 60-inch lengths

glue stick

5-inch and 8-inch polystyrene blocks 2 inches deep

8 doweling rods

floral wires, cut into 3

*Cymbidium* orchids, Vandella roses, and guelder rose

**1** Place the cakes on their baseboards and cover with marzipan and ivory royal icing, following the techniques on page 129 and 134; let firm overnight.

**2** To make the rosebuds, knead both gum pastes until soft and pliable. On a clean countertop lightly dusted with confectioners' sugar, roll out the pastes very thinly—roughly 1/16 inch—and cut into 1/8-inch wide strips.

**3** Roll up one of the paste strips to create a small rosebud. Trim and repeat until you have 72 rosebuds in each color.

**4** Trace the design from the template on page 155 and scribe it onto the side of each tier.

**5** Fit the pastry bag with the tip and fill with ivory royal icing. Pipe a trail of pearls around the base of each tier. Pipe the scribed design onto the sides. Use royal icing to fix the rosebuds, in pairs of each color, in place. Fix a length of ribbon around the edge of each baseboard using a glue stick.

**6** Block the tiers with the flowers, following the technique on page 140. Dress the top tier to finish.

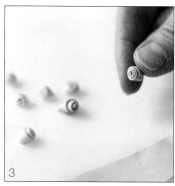
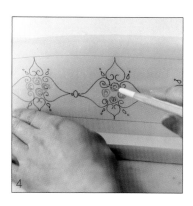
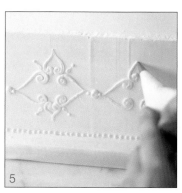

# VINTAGE ROSE CROWN

*Many bridal gowns make good use of vintage lace and covered buttons. I was inspired by the Spanish designer Rosa Clara for this design, with topaz-lustered detail on a four-tier stacked ivory wedding cake. I have crowned this cake with a vintage-style tiara and delicately scented garden roses.*

## YOU WILL NEED

6-inch, 8-inch, 10-inch, and 12-inch round cakes

6-inch, 8-inch, 10-inch, 12-inch, and 15-inch thick round cake boards

marzipan, for the cakes (see page 129 for quantities)

ivory rolled fondant, for the cakes and baseboard (see pages 130 and 131 for quantities)

4 feet ivory ribbon ⅝ inch wide

glue stick

3¼ yards ivory ribbon ½ inch wide, cut into 20-inch, 26-inch, 32-inch, and 39-inch lengths

sharp scissors

1 quantity royal icing (see page 133), colored with concentrated ivory edible food color

18 doweling rods

scribe

2 pastry bags

nos. 1.5 and 4 tips

15-inch diameter cake stand

David Austin scented white garden roses

tiara

**1** Place the cakes on cake boards of the same size and cover with marzipan and ivory rolled fondant, following the techniques on pages 128 and 130–1. Cover the largest cake board (the baseboard) with ivory rolled fondant, following the technique on page 130; let firm overnight.

**2** Fix the length of ⅝-inch ribbon around the edge of the baseboard using a glue stick. Wrap a length of ½-inch ribbon around the base of each tier, trim neatly, and hold in position with a dab of royal icing. Stack the tiers, following the technique on page 141.

**3** Using the picture opposite as a guide, scribe the design onto the second and third tiers to create a scalloped effect. Scribe the outline of the panels on the base tier. Fit the pastry bags with the tips and fill with ivory royal icing. Use the no. 1.5 tip to pipe a filigree edge to the design and fill in with cornelli piping (an elaborate lacelike pattern; see detail on page 52). Repeat this technique with the panels on the base tier and edge these with a pearl trail.

**4** Use the no. 4 tip to pipe a vertical trail of pearl "buttons" down the center of the design.

**5** Pipe delicate pearls above the ribbon edge at regular ½-inch intervals on every tier.

**6** Place the cake on the cake stand, position a dome of fresh roses on the top tier, and set the tiara in front to hold the roses in position.

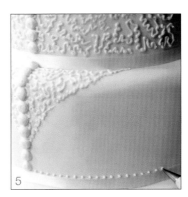

# LACE VEIL

*Lace veils create an ethereal entrance to a wedding. Jasper Conran uses the most delicate of lace in his designs, and I have hand-brushed my own piped lace design on this cake for similar effect. The cake was lustered and stacked offset before the lace veil was iced in place. Fresh roses complete the picture.*

## YOU WILL NEED

6-inch, 9-inch, and 12-inch round cakes

6-inch, 9-inch, and 12-inch thick round cake boards

marzipan, for the cakes
(see page 129 for quantities)

caramel rolled fondant, for the cakes
(see page 130 for quantities)

4 tsp. topaz luster

12 doweling rods

tracing paper and pen

scribe

2½ yards ivory ribbon ⅝ inch wide,
cut into 20-inch, 30-inch, and 39-inch lengths

sharp scissors

1 quantity royal icing (see page 133), colored with
concentrated ivory edible food color

2 pastry bags

nos. 1.5 and 2 tips

white cake stand

3 dusky pink roses

**1** Place the cakes on thick cake boards of the same size and cover with marzipan and caramel rolled fondant, following the techniques on pages 128 and 130–1. Rub the topaz luster over the top and sides of all the tiers; let firm overnight.

**2** Stack the tiers, following the technique on page 141, but offset toward the back rather than placed centrally.

**3** Trace the design from the template on page 152 and scribe the scalloped outline edge to the lace veil, starting on the top tier and trailing down over the 3 tiers. Wrap a length of ribbon around the base of each tier, trim neatly, and hold in position with a dab of ivory royal icing.

**4** Fit the pastry bags with the tips and fill with icing. Use the no. 2 tip to pipe the flower lace design within the scribed veil outline.

**5** Dip a fine paintbrush in water and brush the edges of the design inward to create an embroidery effect. Continue to pipe all the detail within the veil area, then use the no. 1.5 tip to pipe over the scribed lines to mark the outline edge of the veil, with its pearls and fringing (see detail on page 53).

**6** Present the cake on a white cake stand and dress with dusky pink roses.

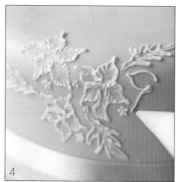

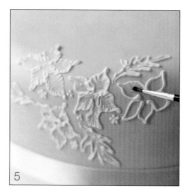

# MANDARIN

*This cake, covered in white chocolate fans and blocked with flowers, was inspired both by beautiful Victorian fans, which were often made from lace with optional fringe, tassels, and marabou feathers, and by their modern-day counterparts of Chinese and Thai paper and bamboo fans.*

## YOU WILL NEED

6-inch, 9-inch, and 12-inch round cakes

6-inch, 9-inch, and 12-inch thick round cake boards

white chocolate plastique (see page 135), for the cakes (see page 129 for quantities), plus 2 lb. 8 oz. for the roses and leaves and 3 lb. 4 oz. for the fans

1¾-inch rose-leaf plunger veiner and cutter

confectioners' sugar, for dusting

small rolling pin

sharp knife

pastry brush

3½ oz. white chocolate, melted

4-inch and 6-inch polystyrene columns 3 inches deep

8 doweling rods

17 floral wires, cut into 3

30 roses, 20 cymbidium orchids, and 2 bunches of lilac

**1** Place the cakes on thick cake boards of the same size and cover with 2 coats of white chocolate plastique, following the techniques for marzipan and rolled fondant on pages 128 and 130–1; let firm overnight.

**2** Use the 2 lb.8 oz. white chocolate plastique to make 30 hand-molded roses, following the technique on page 136 and using 1 oz. plastique per rose, and 40 rose leaves, using the leaf plunger veiner and cutter, following the technique on page 110 and using ¼ oz. per leaf.

**3** To make the fans, knead the 3 lb. 4 oz. plastique until soft and pliable. Lightly dust a clean countertop with confectioners' sugar and roll out the plastique to a depth of ¼ inch. Using a sharp knife, cut a rectangle approximately 8 x 6 inches and form it into pleats, working from one of the long sides. Fold the pleated length in half to create a fan and set aside to firm up. Repeat with the remaining rolled-out plastique until you have a total of 30 fans.

**4** Using the pastry brush, paint the back of one fan with melted chocolate and fix it to the side of the base tier. Continue around the entire tier, using 12 of the fans, then fill the gaps with roses and leaves. Repeat with the other two tiers, using 8 fans for the middle tier and 10 for the top, making sure you cover the top as well as the sides of the top tier.

**5** Block the tiers with the flowers, following the technique on page 140. Dress the top tier to finish.

## TIP

Allow the fans and roses to come just higher than the top of each cake so the fresh flowers tuck through nicely when the cake is blocked.

# CHOCOLATE ROSE POLKA DOT

*Polka dots have always been fashionable, youthful, and fun. They may be used in a contrasting color for a more dramatic effect, or tonal as I have chosen for this cake—very much in the style of a jacquard weave. The tiers have been gently raised and the gaps blocked with hand-molded white chocolate roses.*

## YOU WILL NEED

6-inch, 9-inch, 12-inch, and 15-inch round cakes

6-inch, 9-inch, 12-inch, 15-inch, and 18-inch thick round cake boards

38 lb. 4 oz. white chocolate plastique (see page 135)— 28 lb. 8 oz. for the cakes, 5 lb. for the board, 4 lb. 8 oz. for the roses, and 3½ oz. for the polka dots

5½ yards cream grosgrain ribbon ⅝ inch wide, cut into 20-inch, 30-inch, 40-inch, 48-inch and 57-inch lengths

glue stick

sharp scissors

royal icing (see page 133), for fixing

confectioners' sugar, for dusting

small rolling pin

¾-inch diameter polka-dot plunger cutter

sugar glue

18 doweling rods

5-inch, 8-inch, and 11-inch polystyrene columns 1 inch deep

**1** Place the cakes on thick cake boards of the same size and cover with a double layer of white chocolate plastique, following the techniques for applying marzipan and rolled fondant on pages 128 and 130–1. Cover the largest board (the baseboard) with white chocolate plastique; let firm overnight.

**2** Fix a length of ribbon around the edge of the baseboard using a glue stick. Also, wrap a length of ribbon around the base of each tier, trim neatly, and hold in position with a dab of royal icing.

**3** Use the white chocolate plastique to make 50 hand-molded roses, 3 inches in diameter, following the technique on page 136, teasing the petals out to make a thinner, frilled edge; let firm.

**4** To make the polka dots, knead the white chocolate plastique until it is soft and pliable. On a clean countertop lightly dusted with confectioners' sugar, roll out the white chocolate plastique to a depth of ⅛ inch. Use the polka-dot plunger cutter to stamp out approximately 60 polka dots.

**5** Position the polka dots randomly over the cake, using sugar glue to fix them in position.

**6** Prepare the cakes for blocking with flowers, following the technique on page 140, but do not add the flowers in step 3. Stack the tiers into position, using some icing on top of each polystyrene column to hold the tier above in position. Add the roses, using icing to hold them in place.

## TIP

Royal icing is stronger to hold the tiers and roses in position than melted white chocolate.

40 2-inch square cakes
(see page 132 for cutting instructions)

marzipan, for the cakes
(see page 132 for quantities)

ivory rolled fondant, for the cakes and the stand
(see pages 132 and 131 for quantities)

8-inch, 10-inch, and 12-inch thick square cake boards

6½ yards ivory ribbon ⅜ inch wide, cut into 32-inch, 39-inch, and
48-inch lengths for the boards; the rest for the blocks

4-inch and 6-inch polystyrene blocks 3 inches deep

pastry bag

royal icing (see page 133), colored with
concentrated ivory edible food color, for fixing

sharp scissors

40 sugar rosebuds with green calyxes
(see page 145)—20 dusky pink, 20 brown

4½ yards dusky pink organza ribbon ⅜ inch wide,
cut into 8-inch lengths

4½ yards brown organza ribbon ⅜ inch wide,
cut into 8-inch lengths

# ROSEBUDS *These delicate individual parcel cakes have been topped with a single rosebud and tied with an organza ribbon in a complementing color. They are perfect for a more intimate wedding or civil partnership and can be served one per guest with Champagne or coffee. Alternatively, they could be taken home as mementoes.*

**1** Cover the cakes with marzipan and ivory rolled fondant, following the techniques on page 132. Prepare a 3-tier iced stand using the cake boards, rolled fondant, ivory ribbon, and polystyrene blocks listed, following the technique on page 139 to the end of step 4; let firm overnight.

**2** Fill a pastry bag with ivory royal icing and snip the end with sharp scissors. Pipe a pearl in the center of each cake and place a rosebud in position.

**3** Wrap a length of organza ribbon around the middle of each cake, matching the rosebud color, and secure with a double knot. Trim the ends with the sharp scissors.

**4** Place the cakes on each tier of the stand, alternating colors, with all the ribbon ties facing outward. Assemble the stand following step 5 on page 139.

## YOU WILL NEED

4-inch, 6-inch, and 8-inch round cakes

4-inch, 6-inch, and 8-inch thick round cake boards

marzipan, for the cakes (see page 129 for quantities)

rolled fondant, for the cakes
(see page 130 for quantities)

1⅝ yards white ribbon ⅝ inch wide, cut into 14-inch,
20-inch, and 26-inch lengths

sharp scissors

royal icing (see page 133), colored with
concentrated ivory edible food color, for fixing

12 doweling rods

4 tsp. cocoa butter

powder dusts in pinks, greens, blues, and white

fine paintbrushes

4 floral wires, cut into 3

12 pale pink rosebuds, gypsophilia,
and forget-me-nots

6-inch polystyrene column 2 inches deep

15-inch diameter cake stand

# PETITE ROSE  *The hand-painted roses and buds on this smaller, three-tier cake can be repeated on several individual cakes for presentation to the bridesmaids or flower girls as mementoes. Beautifully intricate and individual, this cake does not follow a strict template, so the finished result will be expressive and completely unique.*

**1** Place the cakes on thick cake boards of the same size and cover with marzipan and rolled fondant, following the techniques on pages 128 and 130–1; let firm overnight.

**2** Wrap a length of ribbon around the base of each tier, trim neatly, and hold in position with a dab of royal icing. Stack the cakes following the technique on page 141.

**3** Melt the cocoa butter by placing it on a saucer over a bowl of freshly boiled water. Place the powder dusts in a palette and blend a little cocoa butter with each one as needed. (If the cocoa butter begins to harden during the painting process, place the saucer over more freshly boiled water.) Using the design template on page 151 as a guide, paint roses and buds on the top tier and cascading down over the cake to the opposite side at the base. Using shades of pink, blue, and green, fill in with stalks, leaves, tiny blue forget-me-not flowers, and spots; let dry. Wire the roses, following the technique on page 145.

**4** Place the polystyrene column on the cake stand and stud with the fresh flowers. Place the stacked cake on top and dress the top tier with a small arrangement of similar fresh flowers.

fun and funky

# RAINBOW DROPS
*Cute and colorful, these individual cakes are stylish yet funky. Hand piped with bright drops of colored royal icing concentrating toward the base of each tier like Champagne bubbles, they look fabulous en masse set on a stand and served with chilled pink Champagne.*

## YOU WILL NEED

33 2-inch round cakes
(see page 132 for cutting instructions)

4-inch round cake

4-inch thin round cake board

marzipan, for all the cakes
(see pages 129 and 132 for quantities)

ivory rolled fondant, for all the cakes and the stand
(see pages 130, 132, and 139 for quantities)

7-inch, 9-inch, 11-inch, and 13-inch thick round
cake boards

3⅝ yards orange ribbon ⅝ inch wide, cut into
22-inch, 30-inch, 36-inch, and 44-inch lengths

7⅔ yards white ribbon ⅝ inch wide

4-inch, 5-inch, and 6-inch polystyrene columns
3 inches deep

3 pastry bags

3 no. 1.5 tips

1 quantity royal icing (see page 133),
divided into 3 and colored with concentrated
edible food colors as follows: ⅓ fuchsia pink,
⅓ orange, and ⅓ leaf green

7½ yards green ribbon ⅝ inch wide,
cut into 8-inch lengths

sharp scissors

**1** Cover all the cakes with marzipan and ivory rolled fondant, following the techniques on pages 128, 130–1, and 132, and putting the large cake on a thin board first. Prepare a 4-tier iced stand, using the cake boards, rolled fondant, orange and white ribbons, and polystyrene columns listed left, following the technique on page 139 to the end of step 4; let firm overnight.

**2** Fit the pastry bags with the tips and fill each with 1 color of royal icing. Wrap a length of green ribbon around the base of each cake, trim neatly, and hold in position with a dab of icing. Pipe tiny pearls on each cake, concentrating them toward the base of each cake and letting them peter out toward the top.

**3** Place the little cakes on the lower 3 tiers of the stand, with all the ribbon joins facing inward. Assemble the stand following step 5 on page 139 and place the 4-inch cake on the top tier.

# COUTURE CONFETTI

*One of my favorite parts of a wedding is confetti being liberally thrown over the happy couple. I thought it would be fun to create a wedding cake with delicate piped confetti (horseshoes, hearts, and a picot triangle of pearls joined together) photographed with fresh rose petals showering down over it. Et voila!*

## YOU WILL NEED

6-inch, 9-inch, and 12-inch round cakes

6-inch, 9-inch, 12-inch, 15-inch, and 18-inch thick round cake boards

marzipan, for the cakes
(see page 129 for quantities)

rolled fondant, for the cakes and 2 baseboards
(see pages 130 and 131 for quantities)

5½ yards white ribbon ⅝ inch wide, cut into 20-inch, 30-inch, and 39-inch lengths for the cakes and 48-inch and 57-inch lengths for the baseboards

sharp scissors

1 quantity royal icing (see page 133), divided into 4 and colored with concentrated edible food colors as follows: ¼ ivory, ¼ pink, ¼ fuchsia, and ¼ left white

glue stick

12 doweling rods

4 pastry bags

4 no. 1.5 tips

**1** Place the cakes on thick cake boards of the same size and cover with marzipan and rolled fondant, following the techniques on pages 128 and 130–1. Cover the 2 largest boards (the baseboards) with rolled fondant, following the technique on page 130; let firm overnight.

**2** Wrap a length of ribbon around the base of each tier, trim neatly, and hold in position with a dab of royal icing. Fix a length of ribbon around the baseboards using a glue stick and fix the boards together with a dab of royal icing. Stack the tiers centrally on the stacked baseboards, following the technique on page 141.

**3** Fit the pastry bags with tips and fill each with a different colored royal icing. Using the template design on page 152 as a guide only, pipe "falling" confetti on the top and sides of each tier. Insure the top of each tier and the baseboards are well covered with confetti, as they would be if it had freshly fallen, but concentrate the design around the base of the sides of the tiers, petering out toward the top of the sides of the tiers.

### TIP

I found it easier to pipe this design working with one color at a time—going all over and around each tier before moving on with the next color.

# RUFFLE TRUFFLE

*This chocolate sculptural creation oozes rich, indulgent decadence. The cake (preferably the chocolate truffle torte on page 146) is topped with a cone wrapped around with dark chocolate plastique ruffles, filled with chocolate frills brushed with gold leaf. This cake has been heavily glazed and would complement a Versace-inspired wedding.*

## YOU WILL NEED

12-inch round cake

12-inch thin round cake board

white chocolate plastique (see page 135), for the cake (see page 129 for quantity)

dark chocolate plastique (see page 136), for the cake and baseboard (see pages 129 and 131 for quantities, and Tip below), plus 3 quantities for the ruffles, ribbon, and bow

1 lb. 1 oz. rolled fondant

16-inch thick round cake board

1 lb. 2 oz. plain chocolate, melted

6 doweling rods

glue stick

10-inch polystyrene cone 18 inches high

10-inch thin round cake board

3-inch flat paintbrush

large and small rolling pins

unsweetened cocoa powder, for dusting

sharp knife

1-inch flat paintbrush

twenty 6-inch squares of gold leaf

edible spray varnish

52 inches dark brown grosgrain ribbon ⅝ inch wide

**1** Place the cake on the thin cake board and cover with a first coat of white chocolate plastique and a second coat of dark chocolate plastique mixed 1:1 with rolled fondant, following the techniques for marzipan and rolled fondant on pages 128 and 130–1. Cover the thick board (the baseboard) with dark chocolate plastique, following the technique for rolled fondant on page 130; let firm overnight.

**2** Fix the cake in position on the baseboard with a little melted chocolate. Dowel the cake to the top of the tier, following the technique on page 141. Use a glue stick to fix the polystyrene cone to the 10-inch thin board. Paint a little melted chocolate on the top of the cake with the 3-inch paintbrush and fix the cone in position.

**3** Set aside 7 oz. of the 3 quantities of dark chocolate plastique and knead the remainder until smooth and pliable. In sections, roll out a strip 6 inches wide and ⅛ inch thick on a countertop lightly dusted with unsweetened cocoa powder. Trim one long edge with a sharp knife and "feather" the other long edge by rolling it with a small rolling pin until it starts to wave.

**4** Use the 3-inch paintbrush to brush the bottom of the cone and the cake sides with melted chocolate.

**5** Starting at the base of the cake and working before the chocolate dries, wrap the length of chocolate collar around the cake, ensuring the clean, sharp edge is flush with the baseboard. Wrap it right around the base, then start working upward, painting more of the cone as you go, rolling out and adding more chocolate plastique collars until you reach the top of the cake, where you should finish with a flourish.

**6** Roll out smaller strips of chocolate plastique 2 inches wide x ⅛ inch thick and fold them up to create frills. Fix these in position inside the ruffles.

**7** Use the 1-inch paintbrush to lift gold off the gold leaf sheets and dust it on the edge of the frills.

**8** To make the ribbon and bow, knead the set-aside dark chocolate plastique until smooth and pliable. On a clean countertop lightly dusted with unsweetened cocoa powder, roll out the plastique into an ⅛-inch thick long strip and cut out a piece 5 foot x 2½ inches. Cut off a 12-inch length for the bow. Fix the long ribbon remaining around the base of the cake and hold it in position with melted chocolate. Cut the 12-inch strip into an 8-inch and a 4-inch length. Fold the 8-inch strip in half and fix this at the front of the cake, opening up the 2 sides of the bow. Finish with the 4-inch strip positioned vertically as the central element of the bow. Trim with a sharp knife to fit.

**9** Spray all over with the varnish—lightly for a sheen or heavily for a high shine—and fix the piece of grosgrain ribbon around the edge of the baseboard using a glue stick.

## TIP

The dark chocolate plastique layer is mixed 1:1 with rolled fondant, so halve the quantity of plastique given in the chart on page 129.

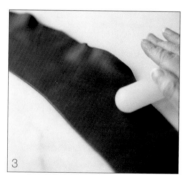

**FLAMENCO** *As the name implies, this cake was inspired by the seductive Spanish señoritas in their black and white polka-dot flamenco dresses, clicking their castanets. I have created this dramatic design with a black frill over one side of the entire cake, which has been varnished with black glitter and dressed with red roses.*

## YOU WILL NEED

6-inch, 8-inch, and 10-inch round cakes

6-inch, 8-inch, 10-inch, and 14-inch thick round cake boards

marzipan, for the cakes (see page 129 for quantities)

black rolled fondant, for the cakes and baseboard (see pages 130 and 131 for quantities)

3½ yards black ribbon ⅜ inch wide, cut into 20-inch, 26-inch, 32-inch, and 45-inch lengths

sharp scissors

royal icing (see page 133), for fixing

glue stick

12 doweling rods

scribe

7 oz. black gum paste

confectioners' sugar, for dusting

small rolling pin

3-inch diameter frill cutter

frilling tool

small knife

¾-inch flat paintbrush

edible spray varnish

2 tsp. edible black glitter

2½ oz. rolled fondant

polka-dot plunger cutter

sugar glue

5 feet black organza ribbon 1½ inches wide

1½-inch decorative button

3 Red Ecstasy roses

**1** Place the cakes on thick cake boards of the same size and cover with marzipan and black rolled fondant, following the techniques on pages 128 and 130–1. Cover the largest cake board (the baseboard) with black rolled fondant; let firm overnight.

**2** Wrap a length of ⅜-inch ribbon around the base of each tier, trim neatly, and hold in position with a dab of royal icing. Fix a length of the same ribbon around the edge of the baseboard using a glue stick. Stack the tiers centrally on the baseboard, following the technique on page 141. Scribe an inverted V from the top to the bottom of the tiers, measuring around 8 inches at the base.

**3** Knead 1 walnut-sized ball at a time of the black gum paste until soft and pliable. Lightly dust a clean countertop with confectioners' sugar and roll the paste out to a depth of ⅛ inch. Stamp out the frill and its center with the frill cutter.

**4** Use the frilling tool to thin and frill the outer edge of the frill. Cut the frill right through at one section so that it opens out into a strip.

**5** Starting at the base of the cake, use the paintbrush horizontally to dampen the cake with water between the 2 scribed marks, around 1 inch from the base of the tier. Line up 1 edge of the frill with the scribed inverted V, with the flat section of the frill uppermost and flush with the cake, frilly side pointing toward the base and frilling away from the cake. Trim the frill to fit flush within the inverted V.

**6** Make more frills 1 at a time to prevent the paste drying out, and lay on top of the previous one so that the flat flush parts are covered by the frilly part of the frill above. Repeat until the entire inverted V is filled with frills. Spray the frills with varnish and sprinkle with glitter.

**7** Knead the plain rolled fondant until soft and pliable. Lightly dust a clean countertop with confectioners' sugar and roll out the paste to a depth of ⅛ inch. Use the polka-dot plunger cutter to stamp out white circles ¼ inch in diameter; fix these randomly over the entire cake with sugar glue.

**8** To make the organza bow, thread 39 inches of the ribbon through the back of the decorative button. Tie the ribbon in a double bow and trim the tails with sharp scissors. Fix this ribbon and bow in position with royal icing at the top of the frill. Tie the roses with the remaining length of ribbon and arrange on the top tier.

## TIP

The frill is constructed from rows of separate frills adhered to the cake to create 1 large frill. Gum paste dries out very quickly, so it is essential that you work on just 1 row of the frill at a time. Keep the remaining gum paste in a sealed polythene bag while you are working.

# CHOCOLATE PLEATS

*This beautifully structured cake features pleats of white chocolate blocked with fresh green flowers. Vera Wang and the Lebanese designer Elie Saab create feminine, voluminous gowns with material folds and pleats, which would complement this cake perfectly.*

## YOU WILL NEED

4-inch, 6-inch, 8-inch, and 10-inch square cakes

4-inch, 6-inch, 8-inch, 10-inch, and 13-inch thick square cake boards

white chocolate plastique (see page 135), for the cakes and the board (see pages 129 and 131 for quantities), plus 2 quantities to make the pleats

52-inch cream grosgrain ribbon ⅜ inch wide

glue stick

3½ oz. white chocolate, melted

confectioners' sugar, for dusting

rolling pin

ruler

sharp knife

pastry bag

3-inch, 4-inch, and 5-inch square polystyrene blocks 1 inch deep

12 doweling rods

floral wires, cut into 3

guelder rose, green hydrangea, green chrysanthemums, and chrysanthemum pom poms

**1** Place the cakes on thick cake boards of the same size and cover with white chocolate plastique, following the technique for marzipan on page 128. Cover the largest cake board (the baseboard) with white chocolate plastique, following the technique shown for rolled fondant on page 130; let firm overnight.

**2** Fix the length of ribbon around the edge of the baseboard using a glue stick. Place the base tier centrally on the baseboard, fixing it in place with a little melted white chocolate. Knead the remaining white chocolate plastique until smooth and pliable. Dust a clean countertop lightly with confectioners' sugar and roll out the white chocolate plastique to a depth of ⅛ inch. Use a ruler to cut strips measuring 1¼ x 4 inches; let firm. Repeat to give a total of approximately 125 strips.

**3** Fill the pastry bag with melted chocolate. Starting with the base tier, pipe a line vertically on the cake and position a pleat in place. Repeat with the next pleat, overlapping the first, and continue until the entire tier is covered with pleats. Repeat with the other tiers; let set.

**4** Block the tiers with the flowers, following the technique on page 140. Dress the top tier to finish.

# GLITTER RAINBOW ROSES
*These vibrant-colored cakes, topped with glitter-encrusted roses, were inspired by John Galliano, who can always be relied on to use bold, bright, vivid colors. Presenting these daring cakes at an all-white wedding ensures they will certainly take center stage.*

## YOU WILL NEED

80 2-inch round cakes
(see page 132 for cutting instructions)

marzipan, for the cakes (see page 132 for quantities)

red, orange, yellow, green, blue, and purple rolled fondant,
for the cakes (see page 132 for quantities);
for the stand (see page 131 for quantities); plus the following
quantities for the roses: 5 oz. red, 6 oz. orange, 8½ oz. yellow,
10½ oz. green, 12 oz. blue, and 14 oz. purple

8-inch, 10-inch, 12-inch, 14-inch, 16-inch, and 18-inch
thick round cake boards

lengths of colored ⅝-inch ribbon for the stand as follows:
1¾ yards red; 2⅛ yards orange; 2⅝ yards yellow; 3 yards green;
3¼ yards blue, and 3¾ yards purple

glue stick

4-inch, 5-inch, 6-inch, 7-inch, and 8-inch
polystyrene columns 3 inches deep

paintbrush

sugar glue

red, orange, yellow, green, blue, and purple edible glitter

pastry bag

1 quantity royal icing (see page 133)

sharp scissors

lengths of colored ⅝-inch ribbon for the cakes as follows:
2 yards red; 3 yards orange; 3¾ yards yellow; 4¼ yards green;
5 yards blue, and 6 yards purple

**1** Cover the cakes with marzipan and rolled fondant, following the techniques on page 132. Make 7 red cakes, 9 orange, 12 yellow, 15 green, 17 blue, and 20 purple. Prepare a 6-tier iced stand using the cake boards, colored rolled fondants, colored ribbons, and polystyrene columns listed left, following the technique on page 139 to the end of step 4; let firm overnight.

**2** Make the same number of hand-molded roses as there are cakes, using the different-colored rolled fondants and following the technique on page 136; let firm. Brush the top of each rose liberally with sugar glue.

**3** Working from little dishes of each of the different colored glitters, sprinkle some same-color glitter over each rose until it is fully encrusted. Upturn each rose to remove the excess glitter.

**4** Fill the pastry bag with royal icing and snip the end with sharp scissors. Pipe a pearl in the center of each individual cake and place the rose in position.

**5** Wrap a length of same-color ribbon around the base of each cake, trim neatly, and hold in position with a dab of icing.

**6** Place the cakes on the tiers of the stand with all the ribbon joins facing inward. Assemble the stand following step 5 on page 139.

creative

# PEARLIQUE

*This design is so simple, yet so effective and is undoubtedly one of my favorites. I was inspired to design a cake that was delicate and feminine and felt fresh and innocent. I have chosen to present this cake with a barefoot charm—no baseboard, no flowers, no cake stand, just a beautiful bridal bouquet.*

## YOU WILL NEED

4-inch, 6-inch, 8-inch, and 10-inch square cakes

4-inch, 6-inch, 8-inch, and 10-inch thick square cake boards

marzipan, for the cakes
(see page 129 for quantities)

rolled fondant, for the cakes
(see page 130 for quantities)

3⅛ yards white ribbon ⅝ inch wide, cut into 16-inch, 24-inch, 32-inch, and 39-inch lengths

sharp scissors

2 quantities royal icing (see page 133)

2 pastry bags

nos. 1.5 and 2 tips

18 doweling rods

**1** Place the cakes on thick cake boards of the same size and cover with marzipan and rolled fondant, following the techniques on pages 128 and 130–1; let firm overnight.

**2** Wrap a length of ribbon around the base of each tier, trim neatly, and hold in position with a dab of royal icing. Fit the pastry bags with the tips and fill with royal icing. Use the no. 1.5 tip to pipe a row of tiny pearls ⅛ inch apart just above the ribbon, then pipe a grid of ⅜-inch long straight lines randomly over the sides and top of the cakes.

**3** Use the no. 2 tip to pipe pearls randomly over the lines to encrust the tiers (see detail on page 80); let set 4 hours or overnight.

**4** Stack the tiers centrally, following the technique on page 141.

# EASTERN PROMISE

*I was inspired by a stunning embroidered and beaded tailored jacket for this cake. The design comprises a lotus flower, regarded as a symbol of divine beauty by Hindus, which is painted on, and then each flower is outlined with piped icing and interspersed with pearls. The entire design is then lustered with gold.*

## YOU WILL NEED

6-inch, 8-inch, and 10-inch hexagonal cakes

6-inch, 8-inch, 10-inch, and 13-inch thick hexagonal cake boards

marzipan, for the cakes
(see page 129 for quantities)

ivory rolled fondant, for the cakes and baseboard
(see pages 130 and 131 for quantities)

4⅛ yards gold ribbon ⅜ inch wide, cut into 24-inch, 32-inch, 39-inch, and 52-inch lengths

sharp scissors

1 quantity royal icing (see page 133), colored with concentrated old gold edible food color

glue stick

12 doweling rods

4 tsp. cocoa butter

½ tsp. turquoise powder dust

fine paintbrush

pastry bag

no 1.5 tip

2 tsp. gold luster

1 tbsp. alcohol dipping solution

**1** Place the cakes on thick cake boards of the same size and cover with marzipan and ivory rolled fondant, following the techniques on pages 128 and 130–1. Cover the largest board (the baseboard) with rolled fondant, following the technique on page 130; let firm overnight.

**2** Wrap a length of ribbon around the base of each tier, trim neatly, and hold in position with a dab of royal icing. Fix the remaining length of ribbon around the edge of the baseboard using a glue stick. Stack the tiers centrally on the baseboard, following the technique on page 141.

**3** Melt the cocoa butter in a saucer over a dish of freshly boiled water and blend with the turquoise powder dust. Paint the 3-sided lotus-leaf design randomly over the entire cake, keeping the leaves close together.

**4** Fit the pastry bag with the tip and fill with gold royal icing. Pipe around the outline of each lotus design and add curly stems to fill spaces. Pipe pearls in between the design to give the cake an encrusted look; let dry.

**5** Dissolve the gold luster in the alcohol dipping solution and use a fine paintbrush to luster all of the hand-piped detail, including the pearls (see detail on page 81).

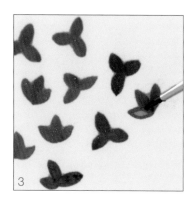

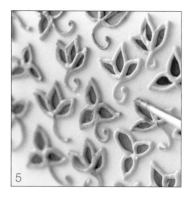

# VERSAILLES BIRDS

*By complete contrast to the monochrome designs in this book, this cake is richly painted with bright, vivid, tropical colors, inspired by the bold and expressive designs of Matthew Williamson and Alexander McQueen. I have dressed this cake with fresh anemones, guelder rose, and green chrysanthemums.*

## YOU WILL NEED

4-inch, 7-inch, and 10-inch square cakes

4-inch, 7-inch, 10-inch, and 13-inch thick square cake boards

marzipan, for the cakes
(see page 129 for quantities)

eau de nil rolled fondant, for the cakes and baseboard
(see pages 130 and 131 for quantities)

3¾ yards deep red ribbon ⅝ inch wide, cut into 16-inch, 28-inch, 39-inch, and 52-inch lengths

sharp scissors

royal icing (see page 133), for fixing

glue stick

waxed paper and pen

scribe

2 tbsp. cocoa butter

wide range of powder dusts

fine paintbrushes

4-inch polystyrene block 1 inch deep

10 doweling rods

floral wires, cut into 3

anemones, guelder rose, and chrysanthemum pom poms

**1** Place the cakes on thick cake boards of the same size and cover with marzipan and eau de nil rolled fondant, following the techniques on pages 128 and 130–1. Cover the largest board (the baseboard) with rolled fondant, following the technique on page 130; let firm overnight.

**2** Wrap a length of ribbon around the base of each tier, trim neatly, and hold in position with a dab of royal icing. Fix the remaining length around the edge of the baseboard using a glue stick.

**3** Trace the designs from the template on page 156 and scribe them onto the cakes, altering the angles and combinations of elements to create variety.

**4** Melt the cocoa butter in a saucer over a dish of freshly boiled water. Prepare a palette of powder dusts, mix a little cocoa butter into each, and use these to paint the design; let dry.

**5** Block the base tier with flowers, following the technique on page 140. Stack the top 2 tiers on the base tier, following the technique on page 141, but offset toward a corner. Dress the top tier to finish.

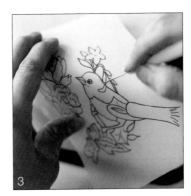

# TREE OF LIFE

*The tree of life is a powerful symbol that appears throughout many different cultures and religions, often relating to immortality or fertility. This striking design was inspired by a glass etching by René Lalique, and its strong lines and eye-catching monochrome scheme create a cake that needs no embellishments.*

## YOU WILL NEED

6-inch, 9-inch, and 12-inch round cakes

6-inch, 9-inch, 12-inch, and 15-inch thick round cake boards

marzipan, for the cakes (see page 129 for quantities)

rolled fondant, for the cakes and baseboard (see pages 130 and 131 for quantities)

4 feet black ribbon ⅜ inch wide

glue stick

12 doweling rods

waxed paper and pen

scribe

4 tsp. cocoa butter

black powder dust

paintbrush

2½ yards black ribbon ⅜ inch wide, cut into 20-inch, 30-inch, and 39-inch lengths

sharp scissors

royal icing (see page 133), for fixing

**1** Place the cakes on thick cake boards of the same size and cover with marzipan and rolled fondant, following the techniques on pages 128 and 130–1. Cover the largest board (the baseboard) with rolled fondant, following the technique on page 130; let firm overnight.

**2** Fix the piece of ⅜-inch ribbon around the edge of the baseboard using a glue stick. Stack the tiers centrally on the baseboard, following the technique on page 141.

**3** Trace the design from the template on page 151 and scribe this on to the cake, starting on the base tier and working up and over the cake onto the top of the top tier.

**4** Melt the cocoa butter in a saucer over a dish of freshly boiled water. Blend with a little black powder dust and use this to paint the design; let set.

**5** Use the scribe to work over the design, etching the detail onto the cake. Wrap a length of ¼-inch ribbon around the base of each tier, trim neatly, and hold in position with a dab of royal icing.

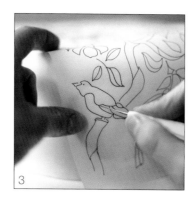

# MONOCHOCCO SCROLLS

*A monochrome scheme can be created effectively by working with white and dark chocolate. Here I have used vertical alternating chocolate scrolls blocked with hand-molded dark chocolate roses and leaves to fashion a design that is both contemporary and chic. It is ideal for serving as a dessert at a wedding.*

**1** Place the cakes on thick cake boards of the same size and cover with white chocolate plastique, following the technique for marzipan on page 128. Cover the largest board (the baseboard) with dark chocolate plastique, following the technique for rolled fondant on page 130; let firm.

**2** Fix the piece of ribbon around the edge of the baseboard using a glue stick. Place the base tier on the baseboard. Fill the pastry bag with melted chocolate. Snip the end with sharp scissors and pipe a generous trail of white chocolate on one side of the cake.

### YOU WILL NEED

6-inch, 9-inch, and 12-inch square cakes

6-inch, 9-inch, 12-inch, and 15-inch thick square cake boards

white chocolate plastique (see page 135), for the cakes (see page 129 for quantities), plus 5½ oz. for the dome

2 quantities dark chocolate plastique (see page 136), for the baseboard (see page 131 for quantity), roses, and leaves

5 feet dark brown grosgrain ribbon ⅝ inch wide

glue stick

pastry bag

5½ oz. white chocolate, melted

sharp scissors

180 white chocolate scrolls

180 dark chocolate scrolls

1¾-inch rose-leaf plunger veiner and cutter

5-inch and 8-inch polystyrene blocks 1 inch deep

8 doweling rods

royal icing (see page 133), for fixing

**3** Place the white and dark chocolate scrolls alternately in position, ensuring they are flush with the baseboard. Continue around the base tier, using 160 scrolls. Repeat with the middle and top tiers, using 120 and 80 scrolls respectively.

**4** Use the remaining dark chocolate plastique to make 100 hand-molded roses, following the technique on page 136, and 100 rose leaves, using the leaf veiner and cutter, following the technique in step 3 on page 110.

**5** Prepare the tiers for blocking with the chocolate flowers, following the technique on page 140, but do not add the flowers in step 3. Stack the tiers into position, using some icing on top of each polystyrene block to hold the tier above in position. Build a small dome of white chocolate plastique 5 inches in diameter and 2 inches tall and place on the top tier.

**6** Using melted white chocolate to hold them in position, place the dark chocolate roses and leaves in the gaps between the tiers and over the dome on the top tier.

6-inch and 12-inch round cakes

6-inch, 12-inch, and 18-inch thick round cake boards

marzipan, for the cakes (see page 129 for quantities)

eau de nil rolled fondant, for the cakes and baseboard
(see pages 130 and 131 for quantities)

waxed paper and pen

scribe

4 tsp. cocoa butter

white, yellow, fuchsia, green, and brown powder dusts

paintbrushes

3¼ yards white ribbon ⅝ inch wide, cut into 20-inch, 39-inch,
and 57-inch lengths

royal icing (see page 133), for fixing

glue stick

12 doweling rods

*Phalaenopsis* orchids

# SPRING ORCHID
*Hand-painted orchids combine beautifully with fresh Phalaenopsis orchids, with their beautiful coloring and delicate structure, although you could use any combination of painted and fresh flowers. The design is clean, simple, and fresh—perfect for a small informal spring wedding.*

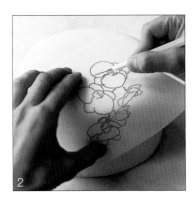

**1** Place the cakes on thick cake boards of the same size and cover with marzipan and rolled fondant, following the techniques on pages 128 and 130–1. Cover the largest board (the baseboard) with rolled fondant, following the technique on page 130; let firm.

**2** Place the base tier offset on the baseboard. Trace the design from the template on page 154 and scribe this onto the tiers and baseboard.

**3** Melt the cocoa butter in a saucer over a dish of freshly boiled water. Prepare a palette of powder dusts and mix a little cocoa butter into each. Use these to paint the design; let dry.

**4** Wrap a length of ribbon around the base of each tier, trim neatly, and hold in position with a dab of royal icing. Also, fix the remaining length of ribbon around the edge of the baseboard using a glue stick.

**5** Stack the top tier on the bottom one, following the technique on page 141, but offset. Dress the cake with fresh *Phalaenopsis* orchids.

# ENCHANTED PEARL

*In 2007, London's Victoria and Albert Museum held an Age of Couture exhibition, where I spotted a pair of gorgeous shoes: sage-green silk stippled with moss green with detailed gold filigree thread, fully encrusted with coral and saffron pearls and beads. They were the inspiration for this enchanted, vibrant cake.*

## YOU WILL NEED

6-inch and 10-inch square cakes

6-inch, 10-inch, and 13-inch thick square cake boards

marzipan, for the cakes (see page 129 for quantities)

sage green rolled fondant, for the cakes and cake board (see pages 130 and 131 for quantities)

6 doweling rods

3¼ yards gold ribbon ⅝ inch wide, cut into 24-inch, 39-inch, and 52-inch lengths

glue stick

1 tsp. cocoa butter

2 tsp. moss green powder dust

flat stippling brush

sharp scissors

1 quantity royal icing (see page 133), divided into 3 and colored with concentrated edible food colors as follows: ⅓ old gold, ⅓ coral, and ⅓ saffron yellow

3 pastry bags

2 no. 1.5 and 1 no. 2 tips

2 tsp. gold luster

1 tbsp. alcohol dipping solution

small paintbrush

gloriosa lilies, Orange Juice roses, and foliage

**1** Place the cakes on cake boards of the same size and cover with marzipan and sage green rolled fondant, following the techniques on pages 128 and 130–1. Cover the largest board (the baseboard) with rolled fondant, following the technique on page 130; let firm overnight.

**2** Place the base tier on the baseboard and stack the top tier on top, following the technique on page 141 but offset toward a back corner. Fix the 52-inch length of ribbon around the board using a glue stick.

**3** Melt a little of the cocoa butter by placing it on a saucer over a bowl of freshly boiled water. Add the moss green powder dust and blend together; use the stippling brush to paint this mixture over the entire cake to form the darker detail. Wrap the remaining lengths of gold ribbon around the base of each tier, trim neatly, and hold in position with a dab of royal icing.

**4** Fit 1 of the pastry bags with 1 of the no. 1.5 tips and fill with gold royal icing. Pipe a filigree of gold over the entire cake. Blend the gold luster with the alcohol dipping solution and paint over the gold filigree piping. Fit another pastry bag with the no. 2 tip and fill with coral royal icing. Randomly pipe pearls over the entire cake. Repeat for the saffron pearls, using the remaining icing bag and no. 1.5 tip.

**5** Place the hand-tied flowers on top.

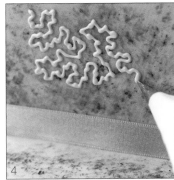

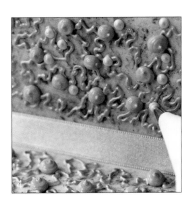

seasonal

# BASKET WEAVE

*A single cake can be sufficient for a more intimate wedding, and I have shown here how it can be presented to maximum effect. Woven leather is popular for handbags, shoes, and belts, so for this design I have decorated the cake with an intricate basket weave in royal icing, with seasonal ways of dressing it.*

## YOU WILL NEED

9-inch round cake

two 9-inch thin round cake boards

marzipan, for the cake
(see page 129 for quantity)

rolled fondant, for the cake and board
(see pages 130 and 131 for quantities)

12-inch thick round cake board

1 quantity royal icing (see page 133)

scribe

2 pastry bags

nos. 3 and 19B tips

39 inches ribbon ⅝ inch wide:
white for spring; pink for summer;
burnt orange for fall;
sage green for winter

glue stick

seasonal flowers and cake stands:
spring—white roses, freesias, and
paper-white narcissi presented on a
white cake stand; summer—pink roses
and guelder rose set on a plinth
decorated with similar fresh flowers;
fall—Orange Brandy and Vandella
roses and oak leaves presented on a
glass cake stand; winter—Grand Prix
roses, calla lilies, and berried ivy
presented on a black glass stand

**1** Place the cake on one of the thin cake boards and cover with marzipan and rolled fondant, following the techniques on pages 128 and 130–1. Cover the thick cake board (the baseboard) with rolled fondant, following the technique on page 130; let firm overnight.

**2** Fix the cake to the covered board with a dab of royal icing. Place the other thin board centrally on top of the cake and scribe around it; remove the board.

**3** Fit the pastry bags with the tips and fill both with royal icing. Begin with the no. 3 tip and pipe a vertical line from the top circle mark to the board.

**4** With the no. 19B tip, pipe a ¾-inch flat basket-weave section horizontally across the vertical line. Leave a ½-inch space below this line and then repeat with another basket-weave section. Continue to the base of the tier.

**5** Pipe the next vertical line ½ inch away from the first, just overlapping the end of the basket-weave sections. Pipe the next line of basket-weave sections horizontally between the previous ones, in the spaces. Continue around the entire cake. Finish by piping a trail of pearls around the base of the cake. Fix a length of the relevant-colored ribbon around the edge of the baseboard using a glue stick.

**6** Dress the cake and present on a stand to fit the season.

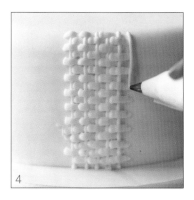

4

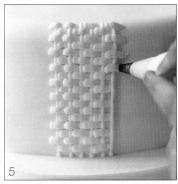

5

# SPRING RAIN

*I was inspired by a bridal gown from the Rosa Clara collection for this cake. Vertical drops of white spring blossom flowers made from sugar are interspersed with clusters of white pearls. I have blocked the tiers with white roses and paper-white narcissi. The design is contemporary, romantic, clean, and fresh.*

## YOU WILL NEED

6-inch, 8-inch, and 10-inch round cakes

6-inch, 8-inch, and 10-inch thick round cake boards

marzipan, for the cakes (see page 129 for quantities)

rolled fondant, for the cakes (see page 130 for quantities)

3½ oz. white gum paste

5-petal blossom cutter, ⅜–¾ inch in diameter

small ball tool

sponge mat

6-inch, 8-inch, and 10-inch thin round cake boards

scribe

ruler

2¼ yards white ribbon ⅝ inch wide

sharp scissors

1 quantity royal icing (see page 133)

pastry bag

no. 2 tip

4-inch and 6-inch polystyrene columns 2 inches deep

8 doweling rods

30 white roses (see page 145) and 2 bunches paper-white narcissi

10 floral wires, cut into 3

15-inch diameter white cake stand

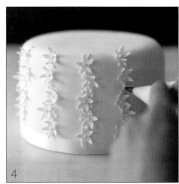

**1** Place the cakes on thick cake boards of the same size and cover with marzipan and rolled fondant, following the techniques on pages 128 and 130–1. To make the spring blossom flowers, roll out the gum paste very thinly and cut out 200 flowers with the 5-petal blossom cutter. (The paste dries out very quickly, so work only a little at a time.) Using the small ball tool and the sponge mat, draw the petals toward the center of the blossom; let firm overnight.

**2** Place a thin board of the same size on the top of each tier and scribe around each to mark a circle on the top. With a ruler, mark 2-inch intervals around each tier and scribe vertical lines at each mark to the top circle line. Wrap a length of ribbon around the base of each tier, trim neatly, and hold in position with a dab of icing.

**3** Fit the pastry bag with the tip and fill with royal icing. Use 5 blossoms per vertical drop and ice these into position slightly randomly and just to either side or on top of the pre-marked line; pipe a pearl in the center of each blossom.

**4** Pipe clusters of pearls between the flowers from the top mark to the base and over the ribbon (see detail on page 98). Continue in this way until all the tiers are decorated.

**5** Block the tiers with the flowers, following the technique on page 140 and interspersing the roses and narcissi. Place on a cake stand and dress the top tier to finish.

# SUMMER GARLANDS
*This wedding cake with pillars is quite traditional, but the garlands of sugar icing, resembling folds of cloth, give it a contemporary feel. The design is reminiscent of a Jenny Packham—style wedding gown, and I have dressed the cake with white lilies, lily of the valley, and white roses—the epitome of scented summer flowers.*

## YOU WILL NEED

6-inch, 9-inch, and 12-inch hexagonal cakes

6-inch, 9-inch, 12-inch, 15-inch, and 18-inch thick hexagonal cake boards

marzipan, for the cakes
(see page 129 for quantities)

ivory rolled fondant, for the cakes and baseboards
(see pages 130 and 131 for quantities),
plus 2 lb. 4 oz., for the garlands

6½ yards ivory ribbon ⅝ inch wide, cut into 24-inch, 36-inch, 48-inch, 59-inch, and 71-inch lengths

glue stick

ivory royal icing (see page 133), for fixing

confectioners' sugar, for dusting

rolling pin

sharp knife

1-inch flat paintbrush

pastry bag

sharp scissors

54 ivory sugar rosebuds with green calyx
(see page 145)

6 doweling rods

6 3-inch ivory pillars

8 white Casablanca lilies, 20 Bianca roses, and 2 bunches lily of the valley

**1** Place the cakes on thick cake boards of the same size and cover with marzipan and ivory rolled fondant, following the techniques on pages 128 and 130–1. Cover the 2 largest boards (the baseboards) with ivory rolled fondant, following the technique on page 130; let firm overnight.

**2** Fix a length of ribbon around the edge of both baseboards using a glue stick; fix the boards together with a dab of royal icing. Position the base tier on the stacked baseboards. Wrap a length of ribbon around the base of each tier, trim neatly, and hold in position with a dab of icing.

**3** For the garlands, knead the remaining ivory rolled fondant until smooth and pliable. On a clean countertop lightly dusted with confectioners' sugar, roll out the fondant to a depth of ⅛ inch. Measure the length of 1 hexagonal side on the base tier and use this as a guide. Cut a rectangle of fondant the same length as the hexagonal panel x 3½ inches high. Fold and pinch the rolled fondant rectangle at the ends to create a garland.

**4** Use a paintbrush to dampen the side of the cake with water where the garland is to be fixed and carefully place it in position. Repeat until you have made garlands for all the sides of the base tier. Make garlands for the smaller tiers, keeping their height at 3½ inches.

**5** Fill the pastry bag with ivory royal icing and snip the end with sharp scissors. Pipe a small amount of icing on the back of the rosebuds and fix 3 at the top of each garland (see detail on page 99).

**6** Prepare the tiers for pillars, following the technique on page 142, then stack the cakes. Tuck the fresh flower heads between the pillars to dress.

## TIP
Make the garlands 1 at a time and keep the rolled fondant in a sealed polythene bag to prevent it drying out and cracking.

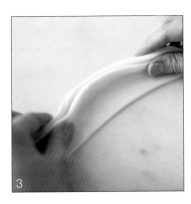

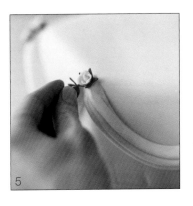

# CONTEMPORARY ROMANTIC

*Sometimes the simplest of cakes can be the most effective. This three-tier square cake is completely plain, effectively forming a backdrop to the flowers and allowing them to shine through. I have showcased four contrasting designs and colors here to complement the different seasons.*

## YOU WILL NEED

6-inch, 9-inch, and 12-inch square cakes

6-inch, 9-inch, and 12-inch thick square cake boards

marzipan, for the cakes
(see page 129 for quantities)

ivory rolled fondant, for the cakes
(see page 130 for quantities)

4-inch and 5-inch polystyrene blocks 2 inches deep

8 doweling rods

floral wires, cut into 3

**1** Place the cakes on thick cake boards of the same size and cover with marzipan and ivory rolled fondant, following the techniques on pages 128 and 130–1; let firm overnight.

**2** Block the tiers with the appropriate seasonal flowers—green *Cymbidium* orchids for spring; peonies, ranunculus, and wired butterflies for summer; Orange Juice roses, ranunculus, and dried lavender for fall; berried ivy and purple anemones for winter—following the technique on page 140. Dress the top tier to finish.

# FALL CHOCOLATE GANACHE AND FIGS

*Aphrodite was the Greek goddess of love, beauty, and fertility, and this decadent cake, made using the chocolate truffle torte recipe on page 146, is packed with the aphrodisiac temptations of chocolate and figs. Rich and seductive, it makes the perfect pudding at a fall wedding served with more figs and a poached pear sorbet.*

## YOU WILL NEED

6-inch, 10-inch, and 14-inch round cakes

6-inch, 10-inch, 14-inch, and 18-inch thick round cake boards

chocolate ganache buttercream, for the cakes (see page 137 for quantities)

6 quantities chocolate ganache (see page 137), for the cakes and base board

ladle

palette knife

57 inches dark brown ribbon ⅝ inch wide

glue stick

12 doweling rods

pastry bag

no. 5 tip

20 fresh figs

30 fresh sage leaves

**1** Place the cakes on thick cake boards of the same size and cover the tops and sides with buttercream.

**2** Before applying the first coat of ganache, place the cakes in the freezer 15 minutes. Remove 1 cake from the freezer and place on a wire rack over a large sheet of nonstick baking paper. While the chocolate ganache is still just warm, generously ladle some over the cake so that it covers the top and gently runs down over the sides. Circle the base of the ladle over the ganache to encourage it to move outward and downward. Firmly grasp the wire rack and gently tap the rack up and down on the countertop to level the ganache and remove air bubbles.

**3** Remove the cake from the wire rack and let set at room temperature. Remove the next cake from the freezer, place on the rack, and repeat the process, reworking the excess ganache from the baking paper. Finally, coat the third cake.

**4** Chill the cakes 15 minutes again. Reheat the remaining ganache either in a microwave 30 seconds or over a pan of simmering water. Remove 1 cake from the freezer and place it on the wire rack. Ladle ganache onto the cake and use a palette knife to spread it over the top and down the sides. Remove the cake from the wire rack and let set at room temperature. Repeat with the other cakes, again reworking the excess ganache from the baking paper. Cover the largest cake board (the baseboard) too and, when dry, fix the ribbon around the edge of the board using a glue stick. Place the leftover ganache in a lidded container.

**5** Stack the tiers centrally on the covered baseboard, following the technique on page 141. Warm the remaining ganache as before until it is smooth, glossy, and spoonable. Fit the pastry bag with the tip and fill with the remaining ganache. Pipe large beads around the base of each tier. Dress the cake with fresh figs and sage leaves.

## TIP

For a smoother or firmer finished cake (especially if you choose to prepare this cake for a summer wedding), replace the first coat of chocolate ganache with a layer of white chocolate plastique (see page 135).

# FALL CANDY STRIPE
*Our candy-striped wedding cake has become an international best seller, and these smart individual versions on their iced stand are just as iconic—so Paul Smith with their vertical stripes in three colors. Each cake is topped with a hand-molded sugar rose and piped green leaves—perfect for a fall wedding.*

## YOU WILL NEED

6-inch round cake

6-inch thin round cake board

35 2-inch round cakes (see page 132 for cutting instructions)

marzipan, for all the cakes (see pages 129 and 132 for quantities)

ivory rolled fondant, for all the cakes and the stand (see pages 130, 132, and 139 for quantities)

8-inch, 10-inch, 12-inch, and 14-inch thick round cake boards

4 yards sage green ribbon ⅝ inch wide, cut into 26-inch, 32-inch, 40-inch, and 46-inch lengths

4-inch, 5-inch, and 6-inch polystyrene blocks 3 inches deep

7½ yards ivory ribbon ⅝ inch wide

12 oz. apricot rolled fondant

12 oz. burnt orange rolled fondant

4 pastry bags

3 no. 3 tips

1 quantity royal icing (see page 133), divided into 4 and colored with concentrated edible food colors as follows: ¼ apricot, ¼ burnt orange, and ½ sage green

silicone parchment or waxed paper cut into thirty-five 3-inch squares

sharp scissors

hypericum berries and Leonida roses

**1** Put the large cake on a thin board. Cover all the cakes with marzipan and ivory rolled fondant, following the techniques on pages 128, 130–1, and 132. Construct a 4-tier iced stand using the cake boards, ivory rolled fondant, sage green ribbon, polystyrene blocks, and ivory ribbon listed left, following the technique on page 139 to the end of step 4; let firm overnight.

**2** Make 35 hand-molded rolled fondant roses (17 apricot and 18 burnt orange) following the technique on page 136; let firm. Fit 3 of the pastry bags with tips and fill each with a different-colored icing. Place each individual cake on a parchment or waxed paper square and the top tier on the smallest covered cake board. Pipe alternating colored vertical lines from the top to the base of each cake.

**3** Fill the remaining pastry bag with sage green icing and snip a V at the end of the pastry bag. With an up-and-down motion, pressure-pipe 3 green leaves on the top of each individual cake.

**4** Set a hand-molded rose in the center of the leaves; let set.

**5** Place the little cakes on the lower 3 tiers of the stand. Assemble the stand following step 5 on page 139. Dress between the cakes with fresh hypericum berries and dress the top tier with fresh roses and berries to finish.

# WINTER SNOWFLAKES

*Winter weddings are becoming more popular, and for this cake I wanted to show an alternative to the traditional Christmas colors of white, dark green, and red. These positively icy square cakes have been covered in either lilac or rich purple rolled fondant, then decorated with jeweled snowflakes in purple and silver.*

## YOU WILL NEED

6-inch round cake

6-inch thin round cake board

35 2-inch square cakes (see page 132 for cutting instructions)

marzipan, for all the cakes (see pages 129 and 132 for quantities)

lilac and purple rolled fondant, for half the cakes each and also the large cake (see pages 130 and 132 for quantities)

9-inch, 11-inch, 13-inch, and 15-inch thick round cake boards

lilac rolled fondant, for the stand (see page 131 for quantities)

16 yards purple ribbon ⅝ inch wide

4-inch, 5-inch, and 6-inch polystyrene columns 3 inches deep

3 pastry bags

1 no.1.5 and 2 no. 2 tips

1 quantity royal icing (see page 133), divided into 3 and colored with concentrated edible food colors as follows: ⅓ gray, ⅓ lilac, and ⅓ purple

4¼ yards lilac ribbon ⅝ inch wide

sharp scissors

waxed paper and pen

scribe

1 tsp. silver luster

2 tsp. alcohol dipping solution

paintbrush

**1** Put the large cake on a thin board. Cover all the cakes with marzipan and rolled fondant, following the techniques on pages 128, 130–1, and 132. Prepare a 4-tier iced stand, using the cake boards, rolled fondant, 12 yards of the purple ribbon, and polystyrene columns listed left, following the technique on page 139 to the end of step 4; let firm overnight.

**2** Fit the pastry bags with the tips and fill with royal icing as follows: no. 1.5 with gray, no. 2 with lilac, and no. 2 with purple. Wrap the remaining purple ribbon around the base of 18 small cakes and the lilac ribbon around the base of 17 small cakes, using 8 inches per cake, and the large cake, trim neatly, and hold in position with a dab of icing.

**3** On the top tier, pipe a collection of trees randomly around the side of the cake and top some with a piped star, using the 1.5 tip and gray icing.

**4** Trace the snowflake design from the template on page 152 and use this as a guide to mark the 6 points of the snowflake onto the top of each small cake with a scribe. Pipe a gray pearl in the center, then work outward with the pearl design, using purple on the lilac cakes and lilac on the purple cakes; let set.

**5** Dissolve the silver luster in the alcohol dipping solution and paint the mixture onto all the gray trees and pearls.

**6** Place the little cakes on the lower 3 tiers of the stand, alternating the colors, and with all the ribbon joins facing inward. Assemble the stand and place the 6-inch cake on the top tier.

## TIP

The alcohol dipping solution evaporates as you use it, so you may need to add more as you paint.

# WINTER TRICOLOR ROSEBUD

*Chocolate has an affinity with winter weddings—lashings of rich dark chocolate truffle torte layered with chocolate ganache buttercream and covered in smooth chocolate. For this winter wedding cake I have tiered white, milk, and dark chocolate and dressed the cake with clusters of tricolor chocolate rosebuds and leaves.*

## YOU WILL NEED

4-inch, 7-inch, and 10-inch round cakes

4-inch, 7-inch, and 10-inch thick round cake boards

white chocolate plastique (see page 135), for the first coat on all the cakes and the second coat on the top tier (see page 129 for quantities), plus 3 oz. for the rosebuds and leaves

milk chocolate plastique (made by mixing white and dark chocolate plastique [see page 136] together), for the second coat on the middle tier (see page 129 for quantities), plus 3 oz. for the rosebuds and leaves

dark chocolate plastique, for the second coat on the base tier (see page 129 for quantities), plus 3 oz. for the rosebuds and leaves

sharp knife

confectioners' sugar or unsweetened cocoa powder, for dusting

rolling pin

¾-inch rose-leaf plunger veiner and cutter

2 oz. each white, milk, and semisweet chocolate

3 pastry bags

14 inches cream grosgrain ribbon ⅝ inch wide

22 inches brown grosgrain ribbon ⅝ inch wide

32 inches dark brown grosgrain ribbon ⅝ inch wide

sharp scissors

12 doweling rods

10-inch diameter glass cake stand

**1** Place the cakes on thick cake boards of the same size and cover with a first coat of white chocolate plastique and a second coat of the relevant chocolate plastique, following the techniques for marzipan and rolled fondant on pages 128 and 130–1; let firm overnight.

**2** To make the rosebuds, warm a hazelnut-size piece of chocolate plastique in your hands. Roll into a ball and flatten with the base of your hand to a diameter of 1¼ inches. Gently curl and roll the disc into a rosebud and trim the base with a sharp knife. Repeat to make 15 of each color chocolate.

**3** On a clean countertop lightly dusted with confectioners' sugar or unsweetened cocoa powder, depending on which color plastique you are using, roll out the remaining plastique to a depth of ⅛ inch. Use the rose-leaf plunger veiner and cutter to mark and stamp out the rose leaves. Pinch the base of each leaf and curl gently downward to create shape and movement. Repeat to make 15 of each color chocolate; let firm.

**4** Melt the three chocolates separately and pour into 3 separate pastry bags. Wrap a length of same-color ribbon around the base of each tier, trim neatly, and hold in position with a dab of melted chocolate of the same color. Stack the cakes centrally, following the technique on page 141. Use the corresponding melted chocolate to fix clusters of rosebuds and leaves on each tier to decorate. Present the cake on a cake stand.

mementoes

# CAMELLIA

*These cakes were inspired by Coco Chanel and the iconic Chanel camellia. I was announced as the Harper's Bazaar and Chanel Entrepreneur of the Year in 2006 and have become very interested in the history of the House of Chanel. These monochrome designs would be the perfect memento for a chic bridal shower.*

## YOU WILL NEED (PER CAKE)

2-inch round cake (see page 132 for cutting instructions)

2¼ oz. marzipan

2¾ oz. black or plain rolled fondant

8 inches black ribbon ⅝ inch wide

8 inches silver ribbon ¼ inch wide

sharp scissors

royal icing (see page 133), for fixing

1 oz. black or white gum paste

confectioners' sugar, for dusting

small rolling pin

¾-inch rose-petal cutter

sugar glue

**1** Cover each cake with marzipan and the black or plain rolled fondant, following the technique on page 132; let firm overnight.

**2** Wrap a length of black ribbon overlaid with a length of silver ribbon around each cake, trim neatly, and secure with a dab of royal icing.

**3** To make the camellias, knead the gum paste until soft and pliable. On a clean countertop lightly dusted with confectioners' sugar, roll out the paste to a depth of ⅛ inch. Cut out 11 petals using the rose-petal cutter. Roll 1 of them to form a central bud.

**4** On 4 of the petals, use the sharp end of the cutter to nick a small amount from the opposite rounded edge and gently soften these edges by rubbing them with your finger.

**5** Dab the pointed edge of each petal with sugar glue and fix evenly around the central bud. Gently curl these petals outward.

**6** Apply the second layer of 6 petals beneath the first layer, overlapping as they go around. Again, gently curl these outward so that the tips are flush with the countertop; let firm. Fix each camellia into position on a cake with a dab of icing.

# GOLD-PAINTED ROSES

*These cakes remind me of heavily gilded Versace designs, with their air of refined opulence. I have served these cakes on gold plates, with gold pastry forks and golden goblets of Champagne. The design would transpose well to the use of other bold colors, such as purple or black, for different wedding schemes.*

## YOU WILL NEED (PER CAKE)

2-inch round cake (see page 132 for cutting instructions)

2¼ oz. marzipan

2¾ oz. red rolled fondant

8 inches gold ribbon ⅜ inch wide

## PLUS

sharp scissors

1 quantity royal icing (see page 133), colored with concentrated gold edible food color

waxed paper and pen

scribe

pastry bag

no. 2 tip

½ tsp. gold luster

1 tsp. alcohol dipping solution

paintbrush

**1** Cover each cake with marzipan and red rolled fondant, following the technique on page 132; let firm overnight.

**2** Wrap a length of gold ribbon around each cake, trim neatly, and secure with a dab of gold royal icing.

**3** Trace the design from the template on page 155 and scribe it onto the top of each cake. Alternatively, set the stencil next to you as a guide and pipe freehand, so each design is individual.

**4** Fit the pastry bag with the tip and fill with gold royal icing. Pipe the outline of the rose; let set.

**5** Dissolve the gold luster in the alcohol dipping solution and paint the rose outline with luster. (Note that this amount of luster paste will be sufficient to paint 15 to 20 cakes.)

# BLACK TIE

*As their name suggests, these cakes would be the perfect memento for a black-tie wedding. I have presented them here in two colorways: black ribbon and bow for the gentlemen and pink ribbon and bow for the ladies. Thin ribbon bows are used by a number of designers, including Anya Hindmarch and Vera Wang.*

## YOU WILL NEED (PER CAKE)

2-inch round cake (see page 132 for cutting instructions)

2¼ oz. marzipan

2¾ oz. rolled fondant

8 inches black or pale pink ribbon 1 inch wide

small sharp scissors

royal icing (see page 133), for fixing

ribbon insertion tool

18 inches black or pale pink ribbon ⅛ inch wide

**1** Cover each cake with marzipan and rolled fondant, following the technique on page 132; let firm overnight.

**2** Wrap a length of 1-inch black or pink ribbon around the bottom of each cake, trim neatly, and secure with a dab of royal icing.

**3** Use the ribbon insertion tool to insert regular slits around each cake, ¼ inch apart, directly above the ribbon. Make a ribbon bow from the length of ⅛-inch ribbon; snip the remainder into ¼-inch lengths.

**4** Use the ribbon insertion tool to tuck 1 end of the ribbon into the first slit, then the other end into the next slit. Repeat around the entire cake.

**5** Fix the ribbon bow in position centrally on top of the cake with royal icing.

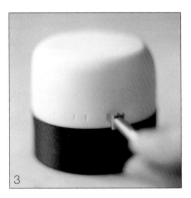

# TRINKET BOXES

*Beautiful jewels make beautiful mementoes, but if we can't all have a beautiful Boodles cocktail ring, as I have shown here, at least you can present your guests with individual trinket-box cakes. These were inspired by Tiffany and Co., but can be recreated in a spectrum of colors to complement any wedding.*

## YOU WILL NEED (PER CAKE)

2-inch square cake (see page 132 for cutting instructions)

2½ oz. marzipan

3½ oz. blue rolled fondant

### PLUS

confectioners' sugar, for dusting

rolling pin

sharp knife

pastry brush

brandy

pastry bag

no. 3 tip

1 quantity royal icing (see page 133)

**1** Cover each cake with marzipan, following the technique on page 132. Knead the blue rolled fondant until smooth and pliable.

**2** On a clean countertop lightly dusted with confectioners' sugar, roll out the rolled fondant to a depth of ⅛ inch and cut a 10- x 2-inch strip. Brush the sides of the cake with brandy and wrap the rolled fondant strip around it. Trim the excess vertically with a sharp knife to make a neat join at the back.

**3** Roll out the excess fondant to form a 3-inch square; cut out a ½-inch square from each corner.

**4** Brush the top of the cake and the top ⅛ inch of the fondant-coated sides of the cake with brandy and place the lid in position. Gently pinch the corners to create a neat box shape.

**5** Fit the pastry bag with the tip and fill with royal icing. Pipe a line from the base of the lid on 1 side to the opposite side; repeat with the other 2 sides. Finally, pipe a bow in the center with 2 tails. Set aside to dry.

# CAN CAN

*Our larger Cannes Cannes wedding cake has been such a huge favorite with our clients that it made perfect sense to create these individual cakes in a similar design, finished with a ribbon and bow to complement. These froufrou cakes, with their appealing frills, can also be made using chocolate plastique.*

## YOU WILL NEED (PER CAKE)

2-inch square cake (see page 132 for cutting instructions)

2½ oz. marzipan

6 oz. rolled fondant

confectioners' sugar, for dusting

small rolling pin

sharp knife

pastry brush

brandy

paintbrush

16 inches ribbon ⅜ inch wide

sharp scissors

royal icing (see page 133), for fixing

**1** Cover each cake with marzipan and half the rolled fondant, following the technique on page 132; let firm overnight.

**2** Knead the remaining rolled fondant until smooth and pliable. On a clean countertop lightly dusted with confectioners' sugar, roll out the rolled fondant to a depth of ⅛ inch. Cut a strip 10 x 2¾ inches—or ⅜ inch taller than the covered cake—and use the edge of a small rolling pin to gently feather one of the long edges. Brush the sides of the cake with brandy and wrap the fondant strip around, feather edge upward. Trim the excess vertically with a sharp knife to make a neat join at the back.

**3** Roll out the excess fondant to the same depth and cut into 3- x ¾-inch strips. Gently gather 1 of the strips to make a ruffle frill.

**4** Dampen the top of the cake with water, using a paintbrush, and place the frill in position. Gather more of the strips and put the frills in place until the top is filled.

**5** Make a ribbon bow from the length of ribbon. Wrap the remaining ribbon around the base of the cake, trim neatly, and secure with a dab of royal icing. Fix the bow in position with more icing.

### TIP

For less rolled fondant on the cake, omit the first coat of white rolled fondant. Instead cut a 2¼-inch square of rolled fondant and place this on the top of the marzipanned cake to act as a lid held in position with brandy. Continue with rolling out the collar for each cake.

# BOOTS AND HANDBAGS

*What is couture without the obligatory accessories of handbag and shoes to complete an outfit—or indeed to inspire one? While not technically cakes, these cookies are extremely chic in every way: killer-heel boots to rival any Jimmy Choo or Christian Laboutin creations and a contemporary handbag to match.*

## YOU WILL NEED

⅔ cup unsalted butter, softened

¾ cup plus 1 tbsp. golden superfine sugar

1 large egg, beaten

2½ cups all-purpose flour, sifted, plus extra for dusting

zest from 2 lemons

½ cup ground almonds

½ tsp. almond extract

waxed paper and pen

stiff card

small sharp scissors

rolling pin

small sharp knife or craft knife

1 quantity royal icing (see page 133), divided into 3 and colored with concentrated edible food colors as follows: ½ fuchsia, ¼ black, and ¼ left white

4 pastry bags

2 no. 1.5 tips

fine paintbrush

**1** To make the cookie dough, beat together the butter and sugar until light and fluffy. Add half the egg and beat again. Stir in the remaining ingredients. Gather up the dough and wrap in plastic wrap. Place in the refrigerator to rest 20 minutes.

**2** Preheat the oven to 350°F (convection oven 325°F). Trace the designs from the templates on page 154 and transfer onto stiff card; cut out for use as stencils.

**3** On a countertop lightly dusted with flour, roll out the cookie dough to a depth of ⅛ inch and put the stencils on top. Use a small sharp knife or craft knife to cut around them, reversing the boot templates every other time in order to create pairs. Cut out 20 pairs of boots and 20 handbags. Place the cookies on a nonstick baking sheet and bake 8 minutes until golden. Transfer carefully onto a wire rack to cool.

**4** Thin half the fuchsia royal icing and all the white royal icing to a flooding consistency with water (see page 133). Fit 2 of the pastry bags with the tips and fill 1 with fuchsia piping icing and 1 with black piping icing. Pipe the outlines of the boots and bags, including the curly handles for the bags.

**5** Fill the remaining 2 pastry bags with the flooding icing, 1 fuchsia and 1 white, and snip the ends with sharp scissors. Flood the boots and bags outlines, using a paintbrush to nudge the icing into all the corners. Set aside to skin over.

**6** Finally, use the remaining black piping icing to pipe the flap and clasp on the handbags and the studs and laces on the boots; let set firm. Store in an airtight container until needed.

## TIP

The cookie dough can be frozen up to 1 month double-wrapped in plastic wrap. Allow to defrost in the refrigerator overnight. Once baked, the cookies will keep fresh in an airtight container 12 days but are best eaten within 2 to 3 days.

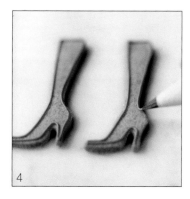

4

4

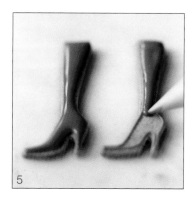

5

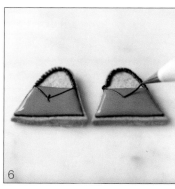

6

# techniques,
## recipes, and templates

# TECHNIQUES

These techniques will help you with covering your baked cakes in preparation for the decorative techniques shown in the chapters, as well as assembling the tiers. There are recipes for icings and fillings, and instructions on making and wiring edible and fresh flowers. Most cakes should be covered the day before you start the final decoration, to provide a firm surface to work on.

## COVERING A CAKE WITH MARZIPAN

It is essential to cover your cake with marzipan or chocolate plastique first. Their function is three-fold: Being oil-based they lock in moisture, they provide a firm, smooth base for a smart finish with your top coat, and they prevent the color of the cake leaching into the icing.

### FOR UNDER ROLLED FONDANT

For a layer under rolled fondant, the marzipan is rolled out and smoothed over the cake in one piece to create softly rounded edges.

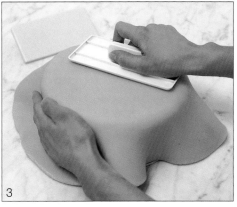

**YOU WILL NEED**

cake

thin or thick cake board of the same size as the cake (see method)

pastry brush

boiled, sieved apricot jam

marzipan (see opposite for quantities)

confectioners' sugar, for dusting

rolling pin

smoother

sharp knife

turntable or bowl

**1** Place the cooled cake upside down on a cake board and brush liberally with boiled, sieved apricot jam. (Note that if the cake is going to be placed on a baseboard for display, as on page 130, then the cake board can be thin; otherwise it should be thick to give stability for stacking or blocking the cake.)

**2** Knead the marzipan until smooth and pliable. Dust a clean countertop lightly with confectioners' sugar and roll the marzipan evenly into a size large enough to cover the top and sides of the cake, allowing for surplus (use string to measure). The marzipan should be approximately ¼ inch thick. Carefully lift the marzipan onto the cake.

**3** Smooth the top and sides of the cake using your hands and a smoother. Trim off most of the excess marzipan with a sharp knife.

**4** Lift the cake and board onto a turntable or upturned bowl and neatly trim the remaining excess marzipan, keeping it flush with the bottom of the board.

## FOR UNDER ROYAL ICING

Cakes covered with royal icing should have sharp, clean, angular edges, so the marzipan needs to be rolled out and applied as separate pieces. This method is more time consuming, but the finished result is well worth it.

**YOU WILL NEED**

cake

baseboard (thick cake board 3 inches larger than the cake)

pastry brush

boiled, sieved apricot jam

marzipan (see below for quantities)

confectioners' sugar, for dusting

rolling pin

sharp knife

**1** Place the cooled cake upside down in the center of the cake board and brush liberally with boiled, sieved apricot jam. Knead the marzipan until smooth and pliable. Dust a clean countertop lightly with confectioners' sugar and roll the marzipan evenly into a size large enough to cut out the top and sides separately and accurately (use string or a ruler to measure), using a sharp knife. The marzipan should be approximately ¼ inch thick.

**2** Using both hands, carefully lift the marzipan onto the cake. Fix the top in position first, then apply each of the sides in turn; trim any excess. Let set overnight before applying the royal icing (see page 134).

**TIP** If the cake is very domed, slice the peak off to level the surface before you turn the cake upside down. You can roll a thin sausage of marzipan and use this to build up any uneven edges around the base of the cake once it is on the cake board.

2

guide to quantities to cover cakes with marzipan/chocolate plastique

● round cake  ■ square cake

| size of cake | 4 in. ● | 4 in. ■ | 6 in. ● | 6 in. ■ | 8 in. ● | 8 in. ■ | 9 in. ● | 9 in. ■ | 10 in. ● | 10 in. ■ | 12 in. ● | 12 in. ■ | 14 in. ● | 14 in. ■ | 16 in. ● | 16 in. ■ |
|---|---|---|---|---|---|---|---|---|---|---|---|---|---|---|---|---|
| quantity | 14 oz. | 1 lb. 2 oz. | 1 lb. 5 oz. | 1 lb. 10 oz. | 1 lb. 12 oz. | 2 lb. 4 oz. | 2 lb. 4 oz. | 2 lb. 12 oz. | 2 lb. 12 oz. | 3 lb. 8 oz. | 3 lb. 8 oz. | 4 lb. 8 oz. | 5 lb. | 5 lb. 13 oz. | 6 lb. 4 oz. | 6 lb. 10 oz. |

# COVERING A BASEBOARD
# AND/OR A CAKE WITH ROLLED FONDANT

Rolled out and smoothed over a cake, rolled fondant creates a fast, clean, smooth finish with gently curved edges. It provides a good base for decoration or looks fabulous simply adorned with flowers. It is soft and pliable, sets firm but not rock hard, and cuts easily.

| guide to quantities to cover cakes with rolled fondant | | | | | | | | | | | | | ● round cake ■ square cake |
|---|---|---|---|---|---|---|---|---|---|---|---|---|---|
| | ● | ■ | ● | ■ | ● | ■ | ● | ■ | ● | ■ | ● | ■ | ● | ■ |
| size of cake | 6 in. | 6 in. | 8 in. | 8 in. | 9 in. | 9 in. | 10 in. | 10 in | 12 in. | 12 in. | 14 in. | 14 in. | 16 in. | 16 in. |
| quantity | 1 lb. 10 oz. | 1 lb. 14 oz. | 2 lb. 4 oz. | 2 lb. 12 oz. | 2 lb. 12 oz. | 3 lb. 8 oz. | 3 lb. 8 oz. | 4 lb. | 4 lb. 10 oz. | 5 lb. 3 oz. | 6 lb. | 6 lb. 10 oz. | 7 lb. 3 oz. | 7 lb. 11 oz. |

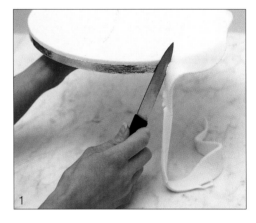

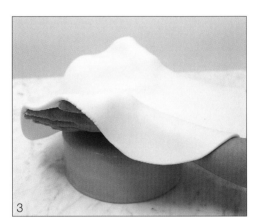

## YOU WILL NEED

baseboard (a thick cake board 3 inches larger than the cake)

pastry brush

cooled boiled water

confectioners' sugar, for dusting

rolled fondant (see opposite and above for quantities)

rolling pin

smoother

sharp knife

cake placed on a thin board of the same size and marzipanned (see page 128)

brandy (optional)

turntable or bowl

royal icing (see page 133), for fixing

metal spatula

**1** To cover a baseboard, brush it with cooled boiled water. On a clean countertop lightly dusted with confectioners' sugar (too much will dry the rolled fondant), knead the rolled fondant until smooth and pliable. Roll the fondant evenly to the correct size—large enough to cover the board and roughly ⅛ inch thick. Carefully place the fondant over the board and use a smoother to finish. Hold the board in one hand and use a sharp knife to cut away the excess, keeping the knife flush with the side of the board; let set (ideally overnight).

**2** To cover a marzipan- or chocolate plastique-covered cake, brush the cake with brandy or cooled boiled water. This acts as a good antiseptic seal between the marzipan and rolled fondant as well as being an adhesive.

**3** On a clean countertop lightly dusted with confectioners' sugar, knead the fondant until smooth and pliable. Roll the fondant evenly into a size large enough to cover the top and sides of the cake, allowing for surplus (use string to measure). It should be approximately ¼ inch thick. Carefully lift the fondant onto the marzipan-covered cake.

guide to quantities to cover baseboards with rolled fondant/chocolate plastique

● round board ■ square board

| size of board | 7 in. ● | 7 in. ■ | 8 in. ● | 8 in. ■ | 9 in. ● | 9 in. ■ | 10 in. ● | 10 in. ■ | 11 in. ● | 11 in. ■ | 12 in. ● | 12 in. ■ | 13 in. ● | 13 in. ■ | 14 in. ● | 14 in. ■ |
|---|---|---|---|---|---|---|---|---|---|---|---|---|---|---|---|---|
| quantity | 11 oz. | 14 oz. | 15 oz. | 1 lb. 3 oz. | 1 lb. 4 oz. | 1 lb. 8 oz. | 1 lb. 7 oz. | 1 lb. 13 oz. | 1 lb. 12 oz. | 2 lb. 4 oz. | 2 lb. 2 oz. | 2 lb. 12 oz. | 2 lb. 12 oz. | 3 lb. 2 oz. | 3 lb. | 3 lb. 8 oz. |

| size of board | 15 in. ● | 15 in. ■ | 16 in. ● | 16 in. ■ | 18 in. ● | 18 in. ■ | 20 in. ● | 20 in. ■ | 22 in. ● | 22 in. ■ |
|---|---|---|---|---|---|---|---|---|---|---|
| quantity | 3 lb. 5 oz. | 4 lb. 3 oz. | 3 lb. 12 oz. | 4 lb. 8 oz. | 5 lb. | 6 lb. | 5 lb. 12 oz. | 8 lb. 12 oz. | 6 lb. 15 oz. | 9 lb. |

**4** Smooth the top and sides with your hands, carefully pressing the rolled fondant against the cake. Be careful not to drag the icing down the sides of the cake, as this will cause it to crack and tear.

**5** Use a smoother to give the cake a professional, clean finish and prick any air bubbles with a pin. Trim most of the excess fondant away from the cake.

**6** Lift the cake onto a turntable or upturned bowl and neatly trim away all the excess rolled fondant using a sharp knife, keeping the knife flush with the bottom of the thin board.

**7** Put a dab of royal icing on the covered baseboard. Slide a metal spatula carefully underneath the cake and thin board and lift from underneath using both hands. Carefully set the cake in position on the baseboard.

## COVERING SMALL CAKES WITH MARZIPAN

Individual cakes need to be covered with marzipan and rolled fondant before they are decorated. Small round cakes are stamped out from a large cake with a 2-inch cutter; 2-inch square cakes are cut from a large cake with a sharp knife. Use 1 layer of a chocolate or lime and coconut cake, split and filled; half a fruit or sticky date cake; or half a lemon or carrot cake, split and filled.

**1** Brush the cake sides and top with boiled, slightly cooled apricot jam.

**2** Roll out the marzipan (2¼ oz. per round cake; 2¼ oz. per square cake) to ⅛ inch thick and cut into 6-inch squares. Place a square over each cake and press down all the way round.

**3** Carefully position a 2½-inch cutter over the cake and stamp out. Remove the excess marzipan. Use 2 straight-edge smoothers together to flatten the top and neaten the sides and base edge.

## COVERING SMALL CAKES WITH ROLLED FONDANT

Once they have been covered with either a layer of marzipan or a layer of white chocolate plastique (for those people who dislike marzipan), small cakes are covered with a top coat of rolled fondant. This will set firm overnight to allow handling and additional decoration. Allow 3 oz. rolled fondant per 2-inch round cake and 3½ oz. per 2-inch square cake.

**1** Brush the marzipan-covered cakes with brandy or cooled boiled water.

**2** Roll out the rolled fondant to ⅛ inch thick and cut into 8 inch squares. Place a square over each cake and press down all the way around.

**3** Carefully position a 3-inch cutter over the cake and stamp out. Remove the excess rolled fondant. Use 2 straight-edge smoothers together to flatten the top and neaten the sides and base edge.

## ROYAL ICING

Royal icing is not only traditional—it is also staging a comeback! Made from fresh egg white and confectioners' sugar, royal icing is a sweet paste that is lathered onto the cake and allowed to set. Once made, royal icing will keep fresh in an airtight container up to 7 days, though it will separate if left for longer than 24 hours and should be rewhisked before using. To color royal icing, dip a cocktail stick into the required concentrated food color, add to the icing, and blend.

**yields 14 oz.**
### YOU WILL NEED (FOR PIPING)

1 large egg white

2¾ cups confectioners' sugar, sifted

juice of ½ lemon, strained through a tea strainer

Place the egg white in a clean, grease-free bowl and whisk until it forms very soft peaks. Add the confectioners' sugar and whisk slowly at first until all the sugar is incorporated, then on full speed 1 minute until it is glossy. Add the lemon juice and whisk another minute.

**yields 14 oz.**
### YOU WILL NEED (FOR COVERING)

1 large egg white

2¾ cups confectioners' sugar, sifted

1 tsp. glycerine

Make as for piping icing, adding glycerine instead of lemon juice. This will allow the icing to be cut without splintering.

**TIP** Reconstituted albumen powder can be substituted for fresh egg white and is available from specialist cake suppliers. It should be used according to the manufacturer's instructions, but the ratio is generally 1 oz. albumen powder and ⅔ cup water to 7¼ cups confectioners' sugar.

## FLOODING ICING

Flooding icing is used to fill the royal iced outlines for making run-outs.

To make flooding icing, you need to thin royal icing down with drops of egg white or water. (Egg white will make the finished run-out stronger, but the icing may take longer to dry. Water will enable it to dry faster, but it will be less strong.) Add the chosen liquid a drop at a time and stir gently. Do not beat the icing as you will incorporate too much air and bubbles will appear in the run-outs. To assess when the icing is of the right consistency, stir it and then count how long it takes for the ripples to subside. If it takes 10 seconds, then the icing is ready—any more, and it is a bit stiff; any less and it is a bit runny.

# COVERING A CAKE WITH ROYAL ICING

Covering a cake with royal icing is a much more laborious technique than using rolled fondant, as several coats are required to build the icing up to the desired thickness. It sets very firm and is somewhat brittle to slice, but the finished icing has a wonderfully sweet flavor and a clean, architectural finish that is perfect for particular designs, for example Antique Rose (see page 48).

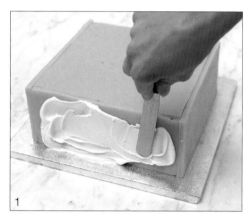  

## YOU WILL NEED

metal spatula

royal icing (see page 133)

marzipan-covered cake on a baseboard (a thick cake board 3 inches larger than the cake)

side and top scrapers

sharp knife

**1** Use a metal spatula to apply the icing liberally onto 1 of the sides of the cake, using a paddling motion to expel any air bubbles from the icing.

**2** Hold a side scraper at a 45-degree angle to the cake and steadily and purposefully pull it toward you. Use a sharp knife in a downward motion to remove the excess icing from the 2 side ends and top edge. Repeat on the opposite side. Let set at least 8 hours before repeating the process on the other 2 sides.

**3** Spread the royal icing liberally on the top of the cake. Using a long scraper and holding the ends away from the cake, carefully pull the scraper at an angle of 45 degrees across the top of the cake toward you. Use a sharp knife to trim the edges. Let set 8 hours in a warm, dry environment. Repeat steps 1–3 until all the sides and the top have received 3 coats.

**4** To cover the board, spread the royal icing onto each side in turn and, holding a side scraper at a 45-degree angle to the board, carefully pull it toward you. Clean the edges with a sharp knife.

guide to quantities to cover cakes with royal icicng          ● round cake ■ square cake

| size of cake | ● 6 in. | ■ 6 in. | ● 8 in. | ■ 8 in. | ● 9 in. | ■ 9 in. | ● 10 in. | ■ 10 in. | ● 12 in. | ■ 12 in. | ● 14 in. | ■ 14 in. | ● 16 in. | ■ 16 in. |
|---|---|---|---|---|---|---|---|---|---|---|---|---|---|---|
| quantity | 1 lb. 12 oz. | 2 lb. 4 oz. | 2 lb. 4 oz. | 2 lb. 12 oz. | 2 lb. 12 oz. | 3 lb. 8 oz. | 3 lb. 8 oz. | 3 lb. 14 oz. | 4 lb. 8 oz. | 5 lb. | 5 lb. 8 oz. | 6 lb. | 6 lb. 10 oz. | 7 lb. 3 oz. |

# CHOCOLATE PLASTIQUE

Chocolate plastique is a combination of pure chocolate with a sugar stock syrup—effectively glucose—which makes chocolate malleable, enabling you to roll it out to cover a cake or hand mold it to create the fans, roses, and leaves used in many of the designs shown here. It has all the taste of chocolate, but with the texture of rolled fondant, and gives a smooth, firm finish to a cake. You can use chocolate plastique to cover a cake in exactly the same way as you would marzipan and rolled fondant. To make milk chocolate plastique, knead together dark and white chocolate plastique.

## PLASTIQUE STOCK SYRUP

**yields 1¾ cups**
**YOU WILL NEED**

1 cup water

¾ cup superfine sugar

6 tbsp. light corn syrup

Place all the ingredients in a saucepan and bring to a boil. Remove from the heat and let cool. This recipe will provide slightly more than is necessary to create the white chocolate plastique recipe below.

## WHITE CHOCOLATE PLASTIQUE

**yields 5 lb. 8 oz.**
**YOU WILL NEED**

3 lb. 12 oz. white chocolate, broken into pieces

½ cup cocoa butter

1⅝ cups light corn syrup

1¼ cups plastique stock syrup

**1** Melt the chocolate in a microwave or place it in a clean, heat-resistant bowl over a saucepan of simmering water. Melt the cocoa butter in a microwave or place it in a clean, heat-resistant bowl over a saucepan of simmering water. (It is important to melt the cocoa butter and chocolate separately, as they melt at different rates and both need to be melted for the recipe to work.) Mix the chocolate and cocoa butter together and stir well. Measure the light corn and stock syrup together and warm slightly in the microwave. (This allows all the ingredients to be at a similar temperature for the final mix.)

**2** Pour the chocolate mixture over the light corn and stock syrups and mix well with a wooden spoon until smooth. Transfer the mixture into a large clean freezer bag and let set overnight at room temperature.

**3** When ready to use, knead the chocolate plastique until smooth and pliable. Roll it out on a countertop lightly dusted with confectioners' sugar.

## DARK CHOCOLATE PLASTIQUE

This paste is quite firm and chewy. Use this recipe for making hand-molded roses, lilies, and other decorations, but mix it 1:1 with white rolled fondant for covering cakes.

### yields 5 lb.
### YOU WILL NEED

2 lb. 12 oz. semisweet chocolate (55% maximum cocoa solids), broken into pieces

4 cups light corn syrup

**1** Melt the chocolate in a microwave or place it in a clean, heat-resistant bowl over a pan of simmering water. Heat to 110°F. Heat the light corn syrup separately to the same temperature. Pour the syrup into the melted chocolate and stir with a wooden spoon until thoroughly combined; let cool completely.

**2** Transfer the mixture into a large clean freezer bag and let set overnight at room temperature. To use, peel away the bag and knead the chocolate until smooth and pliable. Roll out on a countertop lightly dusted with confectioners' sugar.

## HAND-MOLDED ROSES

These versatile and effective roses, which can be made from chocolate plastique or rolled fondant, are ideal for wedding cakes. Use ¾ oz. for a small rose; 1½ oz. for a larger one.

**1** Warm 1 quantity of chocolate plastique between your palms and roll into a ball. (If using rolled fondant, there is no need to warm it first.) Place between 2 sheets of plastic. Flatten quickly with the base of your palm, then, using your index finger, flatten two-thirds of the way around the ball, leaving a thicker base. Repeat to create 4 more petals.

**2** Remove the petals from the plastic sheet and, holding one of the petals by the thicker base, gently roll it to form the center of the rose.

**3** Wrap a petal around the rose center, then fix the final 3 petals so they overlap one another. Gently tease the petals into shape. Slice the base off the rose using a metal spatula.

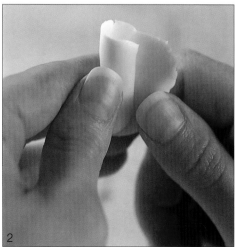

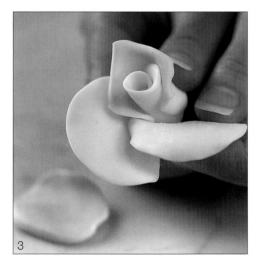

# CHOCOLATE GANACHE

Chocolate ganache is a blend of boiled cream and chocolate. It has a smooth, rich, velvety texture that literally melts in the mouth. Mixed with buttercream, it becomes a wonderfully decadent filling or frosting.

**yields 10½ oz.**
**YOU WILL NEED**

6 oz. bittersweet chocolate (70% cocoa solids), broken into pieces

½ cup heavy cream

Place the chocolate pieces in a clean, dry bowl. Bring the cream to a boil, remove from the heat, and pour over the chocolate. Stir with a wooden spoon until the chocolate is melted and the ganache is smooth and glossy. Pour over the cake while still warm. Alternatively, let cool 15 minutes before making chocolate ganache buttercream (see below).

| size of cake | 6 in. | 8 in. | 10 in. | 12 in. | 14 in. |
|---|---|---|---|---|---|
| to sandwich 2 halves | ½ quantity | 1 quantity | 1½ quantities | 2 quantities | 2½ quantities |
| to cover top and sides | ½ quantity | 1 quantity | 1½ quantities | 2 quantities | 2½ quantities |

# BUTTERCREAM

Buttercream is a combination of softened unsalted butter and confectioners' sugar. The basic mixture can be combined with other flavors such as lime and coconut, orange, lemon curd, and chocolate ganache (see below).

**yields 1 lb. 11 oz.**
**YOU WILL NEED**

1 cup (2 sticks) unsalted butter, softened

4 cups confectioners' sugar, sifted

1 tsp. Madagascan Bourbon vanilla extract

Beat the softened butter for 2 minutes using a wooden spoon or an electric hand-held mixer. Add the confectioners' sugar and beat slowly at first, then add the vanilla extract and beat vigorously until the buttercream is very light and fluffy. Store any excess buttercream in the refrigerator for up to 2 weeks.

## LIME AND COCONUT BUTTERCREAM

Mix together ½ cup grated creamed coconut and the zest and juice of 2 limes. Microwave or place over a pan of simmering water until the coconut melts; let cool. Beat 3 tbsp. unsalted butter until smooth and creamy, then add ½ cup confectioners' sugar and whisk, slowly at first, then at full speed, until light and fluffy. Stir in the cooled coconut and lime mixture and whisk until light and marshmallowy.

## FRESH ORANGE BUTTERCREAM

Stir the grated zest of 2 fresh oranges and 4 tbsp. juice into 1 quantity buttercream. This buttercream works equally well layered in a vanilla cake or a chocolate-based cake.

## LEMON CURD BUTTERCREAM

Stir ¾ cup lemon curd into 1 quantity buttercream.

## CHOCOLATE GANACHE BUTTERCREAM

Stir 1 quantity chocolate ganache into 1 quantity buttercream.

# PIPING ICING

All of the iced designs in this book are created using royal icing (see page 133). Once you have made a pastry bag, just slip a tip into the end, fill with royal icing (colored or plain white), and start piping.

## MAKING A PASTRY BAG

Pastry bags are made from triangles of nonstick siliconized paper. Smaller sizes are good for flooding while larger ones are good for piping single colors onto a number of tiers.

**1** Fold a 12- to 18-inch square of paper in half diagonally to make 2 triangles and cut the paper in half along the crease. Place the paper on the table with the tip of the triangle facing you and bring the underside of the left point to the right of center and hold with your thumb and forefinger.

**2** Bring the right-hand point up, over and round to the back to meet at the center.

**3** Carefully fold the points of the paper over to secure the bag.

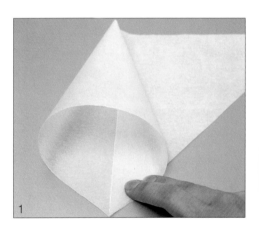

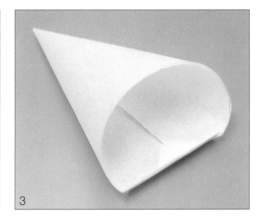

# GLAZING

There are a number of lusters and edible gels available that can dramatically enhance elements of a hand-iced cake. Pearls can be brought to life with edible gel to maintain a dewy appearance, and whole sections of icing can be brushed with lusters mixed with alcohol dipping solution for an authentic sparkle.

## EDIBLE GEL

Made from a sugar glucose solution, edible gel can be brushed neatly onto set icing to create an instant wet look. The gel remains slightly tacky even when set, so be careful when handling the finished cake.

## EDIBLE GEL MIXED WITH LUSTERS

For Queen Elizabeth Diamond (see page 22), I mixed topaz luster with edible gel to create a paste. I then brushed this mixture onto the pearls for an authentic dewy, pearly shine. Various colors of lusters are available, including ruby, sapphire, jade, copper, and gold.

## LUSTERS MIXED WITH ALCOHOL DIPPING SOLUTION

Lusters can also be dissolved in alcohol dipping solution and brushed onto set icing, as on Enchanted Pearl (page 90). The alcohol allows you to brush the luster onto the icing detail (in this case gold filigree) but then evaporates, leaving a matte-sheen appearance. In Bows and Brooches (page 42), the luster is painted over the ribbons, the bow, and its tails, as well as the brooch center. Be careful, though, as the luster will brush off or mark the cake if it is touched.

# INDIVIDUAL CAKE STANDS

Small cakes presented on a stand are becoming increasingly popular and are an effective way to create height and drama for more intimate celebrations. Here I show how to make an iced display stand for small cakes. Stands can be made in many shapes and sizes—round, square, and hexagonal are the most practical. Decide on the number and size of tiers and calculate the quantity of cakes you will need using the chart below.

## ICED STAND

The individual iced cakes shown in this book are presented on iced stands. The color of the icing and ribbon on the stand are coordinated with the cakes.

**1** Lightly dust a countertop with confectioners' sugar. Knead the rolled fondant until pliable and smooth. Working on one of the cake boards at a time, roll out a piece of fondant that is large enough to cover the board to a depth of ¼ inch.

**2** Brush the board with cold water, then lift the icing over the board. Smooth the icing, then, holding the knife against the board, cut away the excess icing. Rub a glue stick around the edge of the board and attach a length of ribbon. Repeat for the other boards.

**3** Rub glue over the polystyrene blocks (for a square stand) or columns (for a round stand) and wrap ribbon around them, starting at the bottom edge and working your way up, carefully overlapping as you go until you reach the top edge. Glue the final piece into place.

**4** Fix each block or column to the board it will sit on with royal icing; let set overnight.

**5** When the cakes are in place, stack the tiers of the stand, securing the blocks or columns to the board above with royal icing to make the stand secure.

**TIP** Make your top tier no smaller than 8 inches in diameter. This will allow the tier below to have a large enough block or column to support the top tier while still providing sufficient space to display the cakes.

### YOU WILL NEED

confectioners' sugar, for dusting

rolled fondant (see page 131 for quantities)

thick cake boards

rolling pin

pastry brush

smoother

sharp knife

glue stick

⅝-inch wide ribbon, to edge the boards and wrap around the central columns

polystyrene blocks or columns

royal icing, for fixing

**guide to quantities to cover stands with rolled fondant** ● round stand ■ square stand

| size of board | 8 in. | 10 in. | 12 in. | 14 in. | 16 in. | 18 in. |
|---|---|---|---|---|---|---|
| ● 2 in. diameter cakes | 5 | 9 | 10 | 12 | 14 | 17 |
| ■ 2 in. diameter cakes | 8 | 12 | 12 | 16 | 20 | 24 |

# BLOCKING A CAKE

Blocking a cake with fresh flowers or fruit is a stunning way to present it, creating an illusion that each tier is suspended on a bed of fruit or flowers. Blocking is also one of the most stable methods of stacking tiers. The polystyrene blocks provide surface-area stability for the tier above and also a base for wired flowers.

## YOU WILL NEED

2 polystyrene blocks, 2 inches deep and 4 inches smaller than the middle and largest cakes

3 cakes placed on thick cake boards, then decorated and edged with ribbon (if using)

8 doweling rods

pen

ruler

sharp heavy-duty scissors or junior hacksaw

**1** Place the polystyrene blocks in the center of the 2 largest tiers. Insert a doweling rod at the center point of each side of the block, making sure they are straight and pushed down to the boards. Mark each doweling rod where it meets the top of the block.

**2** Remove the doweling rods and line them up on a table. The marks will be at slightly varying heights: measure the one with the highest mark and use a ruler and pen to re-mark each rod to this point. (This will ensure the cake is level and supported when the rods are reinserted and the next tier is stacked on top.) Cut each rod to the new mark using heavy-duty scissors or a junior hacksaw. Replace the rods in each cake so that they are flush with the top of the blocks.

**3** Prepare and add the flowers following the technique on page 145. (The flowers are not shown above so that the stacking can be seen clearly.)

**4** Using both hands, gently lift the middle tier and position it carefully on the block of the base tier until it is central, stable, and even. Repeat the process with the top tier, ensuring that the ribbon joins are at the back of the cake.

**TIP** Make sure that you scale the polystyrene blocks with the size of the tiers to maintain stability and to allow sufficient space for the flowers or fruit.

# STACKING A CAKE

Stacking is a preferred American way to present a finished wedding cake. The tiers, which are stacked either centrally over each other or offset to one side or corner, are supported with hidden boards and doweling rods. The overall height of a stacked cake is less than that of other tiered cakes, so for a grander effect you can increase the number of tiers, including some false upper tiers if necessary.

## YOU WILL NEED

12 doweling rods

3 cakes placed on thick cake boards, then decorated and edged with ribbon (if using)

pen

ruler

sharp heavy-duty scissors or junior hacksaw

royal icing (see page 133), for fixing

metal spatula

**1** Push 6 doweling rods randomly into the center of the bottom tier, making sure their line does not fall outside the size of the tier to be stacked above. Use a pen to mark each doweling rod at the point where it surfaces from the cake. (For a large cake such as Queen Elizabeth Diamond you will need 8 rods per tier.)

**2** Remove the doweling rods and line them up on a table. Find the average mark and, using a ruler and pen, mark each of the rods at the same point. (This will ensure the cake is level and supported when the rods are reinserted and the next tier is placed on top.) Cut each rod to the new mark using heavy-duty scissors or a junior hacksaw. Check that all the rods are the correct length before reinserting them into the cake, as they will be very difficult to remove again. Once the rods are pushed right into the cake, spread a small amount of royal icing on the center of the cake with a metal spatula.

**3** Gently lift the middle tier and position it carefully on the base tier. Repeat step 2 with another 6 rods on the middle tier before placing the top tier in position. Adjust the ribbons on the top 2 tiers so they fit snugly against the lower tiers and all the joins are at the back.

**TIP** Leave the cakes for 24 hours after decorating them before attempting to stack them. This allows time for the coverings to harden and set so that you will be able to handle the tiers without the icing cracking or dimpling.

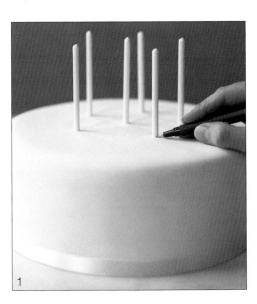

# USING PILLARS TO SEPARATE TIERS

Separating tiers with pillars is a traditional way to add dramatic height and grandeur to a cake, and the space created between the tiers can be dressed with fresh, sugar, or silk flowers. Pillars are available in many heights, colors, and finishes—doweling rods placed inside the pillars carry all the weight of the tiers. With very large or heavy tiers, increase the number of pillars to up to 8 on each tier.

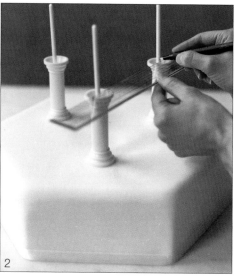

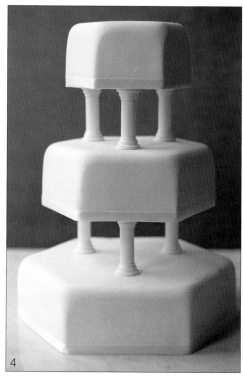

## YOU WILL NEED

grid template (see page 158)

3 cakes placed on thick cake boards, then decorated and edged with ribbon (if using)

scribe

6 doweling rods

6 3½-inch pillars

ruler

pen

sharp, heavy-duty scissors or junior hacksaw

**1** Place the grid template centrally over the largest cake. Select the relevant point to the cake size on a "C" line and mark this with a scribe; mark the same point on the other "C" line and the "A/C" line.

**2** Insert a doweling rod into each of the marked points and drop a pillar over the top. Place a ruler across 2 of the pillars and mark the rods at the top of the pillars with a pen. Move the ruler around to between 1 of these pillars and the third pillar and finally between this pillar and the first pillar, marking the rods each time. Remove the pillars from the cake.

**3** Remove the doweling rods and line them up on a table. Find the average mark and, using a ruler and pen, mark each of the rods at this point. (This will ensure the cake is level and supported when the rods are replaced and the next tier is stacked into position.) Cut each rod to the new mark using heavy-duty scissors or a junior hacksaw. Replace the rods in the cake and position a pillar carefully over each one. Repeat the above with the middle tier.

**4** Finally, stack the tiers, making sure they are level, stable, and centered, and that all the ribbon joins are at the back.

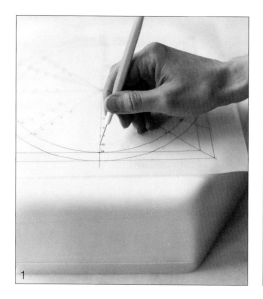

# STACKING TIERS WITH A CENTRAL COLUMN

Separating cake tiers with a central column gives a contemporary, uncluttered look, and wrapping the column in a contrasting or complementary ribbon creates either a dramatic or more subtle effect. It's not necessary to add finishing touches between the tiers, so this technique is popular for designs that reach or cover the top of each tier so that they can be clearly seen.

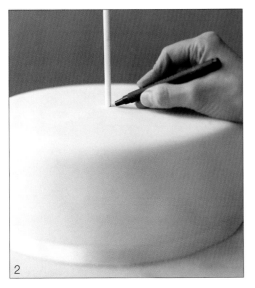

## YOU WILL NEED

grid template (see page 158)

3 cakes placed on thick cake boards, then decorated and edged with ribbon (if using)

scribe

10 doweling rods

pen

ruler

sharp heavy-duty scissors or a junior hacksaw

2 polystyrene columns, 2 inches deep and 4 inches smaller than the medium-sized and largest cakes

ribbon 1 inch wide to cover the polystyrene columns

glue stick

2 thin boards of the same size and shape as the polystyrene columns

royal icing (see page 133) , for fixing

**1** Place the grid template centrally over the largest cake and mark the center point on the cake with a scribe.

**2** Insert a doweling rod into the cake at this point, making sure it is straight and pushed down to the board. Mark the rod with a pen where it surfaces from the cake. Remove the rod and line it up with 4 others. Use a ruler and pen to mark each rod to the measured point. (This will keep the cake level and supported when the doweling rods are replaced and the tiers are stacked.)

**3** Cut each rod to the new mark using the scissors or hacksaw. Push the rods into the cake, keeping them within the diameter of the column. Cover the largest column with ribbon, if using, wrapping it around several times to ensure the polystyrene is covered and securing it in position with a glue stick. Glue the column to a thin board (to prevent the doweling rods pushing up through the polystyrene under the weight of the cake). Spread a small amount of royal icing in the center of the cake.

**4** Carefully place the column on the cake (board side facing down) with the center over the central doweling rod.

**5** Repeat this process with the middle tier, then leave both tiers to set for 30 minutes. Carefully stack the tiers, ensuring the ribbon joins are at the back.

# SUGAR LILIES

Romantic lilies look stunning when used to dress a cake. Here I show you how to make them from gum paste, which will last long after the wedding day. If you want to make pure white lilies, as for Cascading Crystal Rose (see page 44), omit the dusting and painting stage.

 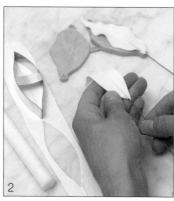  

## YOU WILL NEED

lengths of 24-gauge wire, cut into 3

1 oz. white gum paste

knife

paintbrushes

green and pink powder dusts

large white lily stamens

green floral tape

confectioners' sugar, for dusting

small veining rolling pin

4-inch lily cutter

lengths of 26-gauge wire, cut into 3

4-inch lily-veining mold

soft foam pad

ball tool

brown liquid food color

**1** Bend the top of a length of 24-gauge wire over to form a small hook. Take a piece of white gum paste the size of a cherry tomato and form it into an elongated cone. Pinch the blunt end into 3 to form the end of the stigma and mark with a cross using a knife. Insert the hooked end of the wire gently into the thin end of the stigma; let dry overnight. The next day, brush the stigma with green powder dust. Position 6 large lily stamens around the stigma and tape into position with green floral tape.

**2** On a clean countertop lightly dusted with confectioners' sugar, roll out the remaining gum paste thinly using the veining rolling pin. Place the lily cutter on the paste, centered over the thick vein marked by the rolling pin, and cut out 6 petals. Insert approximately ¾ inch of a length of 26-gauge wire into the thick vein of each petal. Lay the wired petal inside the veining mold, with the wire facing outward, and press the mold sides firmly together to indent the markings on the petal. Place each petal, in turn, on a foam pad and rub it gently with a ball tool, working from the center outward, to feather the edges of the lily gently and give the flowers a sense of movement.

**3** Let the lily petals dry overnight propped over an upturned bowl so that the petals curve gently backward. (For a more closed lily, dry the petals flat.) Dust the center length of each petal with pink powder dust and use a paintbrush dipped into brown liquid food color to paint small dots on top; let dry.

**4** Tape the first 3 petals evenly around the central stamens using floral tape. Add the final 3 petals one at a time and fix in position with tape. Handle the lilies at the base where the wire is inserted, as this is the most stable point.

**TIP** You will need 6 petals for each lily, but, as they're very fragile, it is a good idea to make extra. If a petal snaps, pull it out gently, and tape another into position.

# SUGAR ROSEBUDS

Fingernail-sized rosebuds made of gum paste are delicate and effective yet simple to make. They can be made in more than one color to add interest and contrast to a cake. They keep well if stored in a clean, dry container, so can be made well in advance.

## YOU WILL NEED

½ oz. gum paste per rose –
¼ oz. for the rose (yellow) and
⅛ oz. for the calyx (green)

confectioners' sugar, for dusting

small rolling pin

1¼ inch rose-petal cutter
(5 petals)

ball tool

soft foam pad

sugar glue

⅝-inch calyx cutter

**1** Form a pea-sized ball of yellow paste into a cone; let dry 1 hour. On a clean countertop lightly dusted with confectioners' sugar, roll out the remaining yellow gum paste and press the rose cutter onto it. Use the ball tool on a soft foam pad to gently soften and thin the edges of the petals.

**2** Dab a small amount of sugar glue in the center of the 5 petals and place the cone pointing upward in the center. Gather the first petal up and around the cone, then fold the remaining petals up, tucking each inside the next with one side free.

**3** Roll out the green paste and cut out the calyx. Use the ball tool on a soft pad to gently thin and curl the fronds upward. Dab the center with sugar glue and set the rose in place.

# PREPARING FLOWERS FOR BLOCKING

I like to dress cakes with fresh flowers. There are many varieties and colors available, so it is worth experimenting, but I have found roses to be particularly effective for blocking.

## YOU WILL NEED

florist's scissors

fresh roses

floral wires, cut into 3

polystyrene column(s) or block(s)
2 inches deep if you want just 1 row
of flowers; 3½ inches deep
if you want 2 rows

**1** Trim each rose to leave approximately ¾ inch of stalk. Gently tease a wire into the stalk.

**2** Insert the wire into the polystyrene column or block. Repeat, working around the cake base or tier and ensuring the roses are lined up and equal. (If you are using 2 rows, position the upper row in between the flowers on the bottom row.) Don't underestimate the number of flowers you will need!

**TIP** The table below is provided as a guide only. The numbers will vary depending on the species of rose, how full blown the flowers are, and how tightly you position them next to one another. You may want to include other flowers or greenery to fill any gaps and reduce the cost.

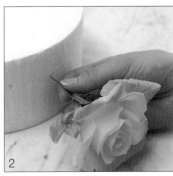

| tier diameter | 6 in. | 8 in. | 10 in. | 12 in. | 14 in. | 16 in. |
|---|---|---|---|---|---|---|
| no. of roses required for 1 row | 8 | 12 | 16 | 20 | 26 | 32 |
| no. of roses required for 2 rows | 14 | 22 | 30 | 38 | 50 | 60 |

# CAKE RECIPES

Choose from chocolate truffle, luscious lemon, moist carrot, traditional fruit, sticky date, and lime and coconut. Note that 1 quantity of cake mixture makes a 6-inch round cake or a 5-inch square/hexagonal cake; other sizes of cakes require multiples as shown in the charts on the right. Cooking times are given in each recipe, with individual increases or decreases for each 2-inch variation on these standard pan sizes.

| cake size | quantities | | cake size | quantities |
|-----------|-----------|---|-----------|-----------|
| ● 4 in. | ½ | | ■ ● 4 in. | ½ |
| ● 5 in. | ¾ | | ■ ● 6 in. | 1¼ |
| ● 7 in. | 1½ | | ■ ● 7 in. | 1½ |
| ● 8 in. | 2 | | ■ ● 8 in. | 2¼ |
| ● 9 in. | 2¼ | | ■ ● 9 in. | 2¾ |
| ● 10 in. | 3 | | ■ ● 10 in. | 3½ |
| ● 12 in. | 4 | | ■ ● 12 in. | 5 |
| ● 14 in. | 5½ | | ■ ● 14 in. | 7 |
| ● 15 in. | 6¼ | | ■ ● 15 in. | 8 |
| ● 16 in. | 7 | | ■ ● 16 in. | 9 |

● round cake          ■ ● square/hexagonal cake

ingredients for 6-inch round cake

7 oz. bittersweet chocolate (70% cocoa solids), broken into pieces

1 cup plus 2 tbsp. (2¼ sticks) unsalted butter, softened

1½ cups firmly packed light brown sugar

5 large eggs, beaten

1½ tsp. vanilla extract

1 cup plus 2 tbsp. all-purpose flour, sifted

bake:  convection 275°F
conventional 325°F

## CHOCOLATE TRUFFLE TORTE

This cake is made with melted chocolate and very little flour, and its texture is similar to that of a chocolate brownie. It's delicious sandwiched with chocolate ganache buttercream. Its low flour content means that this cake is best baked in two halves, then sandwiched together.

**1** Preheat the oven. Have all the ingredients at room temperature. Melt the chocolate carefully in a microwave or in a bowl over simmering water; let cool. Grease and line 2 deep cake pans with nonstick baking paper. Beat together the butter and sugar until light and fluffy. Add the beaten eggs, a little at a time, beating between each addition.

**2** Pour the cooled melted chocolate slowly into the creamed mixture, beating all the time. Stir in the vanilla extract. Fold in the sifted flour.

**3** Spoon the mixture evenly into the pans and bake 45 minutes (plus or minus 20 minutes per 2 inches of pan size). The baked cakes should be well risen with a crust but should still wobble when shaken gently. Remove the cakes from the oven. Let the cakes cool in the pans, then remove. The crust will sink down into the cakes. Sandwich the cakes together with chocolate ganache buttercream (see page 137).

**TO STORE** This cake will keep up to 10 days once covered and decorated or wrapped in waxed paper and kept in an airtight container. It is suitable for freezing, but needs to defrost overnight.

**ingredients for 6-inch round cake**

1 cup plus 2 tbsp. self-rising flour

1 cup plus 2 tbsp. all-purpose flour

¾ cup plus 2 tbsp. (1¾ sticks) unsalted
  butter, softened

1 cup plus 1 tbsp. golden superfine
  sugar

4 large eggs, beaten

grated zest of 1 lemon and 2 tbsp. juice

2 tsp. vanilla extract

**for the syrup glaze:**

remainder of lemon juice (6 to 7 tbsp.)

½ cup golden superfine sugar

bake:  convection 275°F

conventional 325°F

# LUSCIOUS LEMON CAKE

This lemon cake recipe is light and refreshing, which makes it a lovely addition to a summer wedding
and perfect after a rich banquet. Slice it horizontally in half and fill with lemon curd buttercream, then
cover it with marzipan and icing or chocolate plastique. Although there are a lot of fresh lemons to zest
and squeeze, the finished cake is well worth the effort!

**1** Preheat the oven. Have all the ingredients at
room temperature. Grease and line a deep cake pan
with nonstick baking paper. Sift the flours together.
Beat together the butter and sugar until light and
fluffy. Add the beaten eggs, a little at a time,
beating between each addition. Stir a few tablespoons
of flour into the creamed mixture to prevent it
curdling; carefully fold in the remainder. Stir in
the lemon zest and juice and the vanilla extract.
Spoon the mixture into the prepared pan and bake
1 hour 25 minutes (plus or minus 15 minutes per
2 inches of pan size) or until a skewer inserted into
the middle of the cake comes out clean.

**2** While the cake is baking, make the syrup glaze.
Strain the lemon juice into a small pan and add the
sugar, stirring all the time. Heat gently until the
sugar dissolves. Remove from the heat. Once the
cake is baked, remove from the oven and pierce with
a skewer several times. Spoon the lemon syrup over
the top. Let the cake cool in the pan, then remove.
Split and sandwich with lemon curd buttercream
(see page 137).

**TO STORE** This cake is best served and
eaten fresh but will keep for up to 5 days once
covered and decorated or wrapped in waxed paper
and kept in an airtight container. It is suitable for
freezing, but needs to defrost overnight.

ingredients for 6-inch round cake

5 tsp. dark rum

1 cup golden raisins

1½ cups all-purpose flour

2 tsp. ground cinnamon

1 tsp. ground nutmeg

1 tsp. baking soda

⅔ cup sunflower oil

⅓ cup golden superfine sugar

⅓ cup firmly packed light brown sugar

2 large eggs, beaten

grated zest of 1 lemon

grated zest of 1 orange

1¼ cups peeled and grated carrots

⅔ cup shredded unsweetened coconut

½ cup chopped walnuts

1 tsp. vanilla extract

2 tsp. chopped candied ginger (optional)

for the citrus syrup:

⅓ cup firmly packed light brown sugar

juice of 1 lemon

juice of 1 orange

bake: convection 275°F
conventional 300°F

# MOIST CARROT CAKE

This carrot cake with added walnuts, rum-soaked golden raisins, and coconut makes a lovely, lighter alternative to a rich fruit cake. The cake is spiked with a citrus syrup to help keep it moist and fruity. It does not need filling, but some fresh orange buttercream adds a taste of luxury.

**1** Pour the rum over the golden raisins and let infuse 1 hour. Preheat the oven. Have all the ingredients at room temperature. Grease and line a deep cake pan with nonstick baking paper (which should stand at least ¾ inch above the pan to contain the lemon syrup in step 3). Sift the flour together with the ground cinnamon, ground nutmeg, and baking soda. Beat together the sunflower oil, both sugars, and the eggs until smooth.

**2** Stir the flour mixture into the smooth batter. Add the lemon and orange zests, grated carrot, shredded unsweetened coconut, walnuts, vanilla extract, and chopped candied ginger (if using);

stir well to combine. Spoon the mixture into the prepared pan and bake 1½ hours (plus or minus 15 minutes per 2 inches of pan size) or until a skewer inserted into the middle of the cake comes out clean.

**3** While the cake is baking, make the syrup. Place the sugar in a bowl with the strained lemon and orange juice. Stir well and continue to stir at intervals. Once the cake is baked, remove it from the oven and immediately pierce it with a skewer several times. Carefully spoon or pour the citrus syrup over the top. Let the cake cool in the pan, then remove. Split and sandwich with fresh orange buttercream (see page 137), if using.

**TO STORE** This cake keeps fresh up to 14 days if covered and decorated with icing or wrapped in waxed paper and kept in an airtight container. It is suitable for freezing, but needs to defrost overnight.

**TIP** Once the citrus syrup is poured over, it will appear flooded. This is perfectly normal and all this delicious juice will gradually be absorbed into the cake.

# TRADITIONAL RICH FRUIT CAKE

This moist cake contains dried dates, prunes, and apricots alongside the more commonly used currants, raisins, and golden raisins, giving a flavor that is more pronounced and a little less sweet. The molasses gives a rich dark flavor. Ideally, bake the cake 8 weeks in advance.

**1** Combine the currants, golden raisins, California raisins, prunes, apricots, dates, and candied cherries with the brandy and the orange and lemon zest and juice. Let absorb a minimum of 24 hours—ideally 72 hours.

**2** Preheat the oven. Have all the ingredients at room temperature. Grease and line a deep cake pan with nonstick baking paper. Sift the flour together with the ground ginger, cinnamon, and nutmeg. Beat together the butter and sugar until light and fluffy. Add the beaten eggs, a little at a time, beating between each addition.

**3** Stir a few tablespoons of flour into the creamed mixture to prevent it curdling. Carefully fold in the remaining flour. Stir in the molasses, then the soaked fruit (reserving the brandy in which it has been soaked) and the chopped nuts.

**4** Spoon the mixture into the prepared pan and bake 3½ hours (plus or minus 15 minutes per 2 inches of pan size) or until a skewer inserted into the middle of the cake comes out clean. If the top of the cake appears to be browning too quickly, fold a sheet of waxed paper in half, cut a small hole the size of a walnut in the center, and carefully place it over the top of the cake. (Make sure you wear oven mitts to do so!)

**5** Remove the cake from the oven. Let the cake cool in the pan, then remove. Brush the top with the reserved brandy. Wrap the cake in a double layer of waxed paper and a double layer of kitchen foil to store.

**TO STORE** This cake keeps fresh up to 9 months if marzipanned and iced and kept in an airtight container in a cool, dry place. Undecorated, and wrapped in waxed paper and foil, it will keep up to 3 months.

### ingredients for 6-inch round cake

1 cup seedless currants

1 cup golden raisins

1 cup Californian raisins

¼ cup whole pitted prunes, snipped into 3

¼ cup whole dried apricots, snipped into 3

¼ cup whole pitted dates, snipped into 3

¼ cup natural-color candied cherries, chopped

5 tbsp. brandy (40% alcohol)

grated zest and juice of 1 lemon

grated zest and juice of 1 orange

1½ cups all-purpose flour

1 tsp. ground ginger

2 tsp. ground cinnamon

1½ tsp. ground nutmeg

½ cup (1⅛ sticks) unsalted butter, softened

½ cup plus 1 tbsp. firmly packed light brown sugar

2 large eggs, beaten

½ tbsp. black strap molasses

2 tbsp. chopped almonds

**bake:** convection 250°F
conventional 275°F

## STICKY DATE CAKE

This cake is moist, sticky, and full of flavor, and makes a welcome alternative to a traditional fruit cake. It stacks well and requires no filling, making it an ideal choice for the base tier of many of the cakes, though one can be added if wanted.

**ingredients for 6-inch round cake**

1 cup pitted Medjool dates

⅔ cup (1⅓ sticks) unsalted butter,
  cut into pieces

1 cup firmly packed light muscovado sugar

2 large eggs

¼ cup chopped stem ginger

grated zest of 1 lemon

1 tsp. vanilla extract

1 large cooking apple, grated

1⅓ cups self-rising flour, sifted

**bake:  convection 275°F**
**conventional 325°F**

**1** Preheat the oven. Have all the ingredients at room temperature. Grease and line a deep cake pan with nonstick baking paper.

**2** Place the dates in a bowl and cover with boiling water. Melt the butter and sugar together in a large saucepan; let cool slightly.

**3** Beat the eggs, ginger, lemon zest, and vanilla extract into the butter and sugar. Drain the dates and chop finely; add to the saucepan and mix well. Stir in the grated apple and flour. Spoon the mixture into the prepared pan and bake 1 hour (plus or minus 15 minutes per 2 inches of pan size) or until a skewer inserted into the middle of the cake comes out clean with a few crumbs. Let the cake cool in the pan, then remove.

**TO STORE**  Store in an airtight container for up to 1 week. It is suitable for freezing, but needs to defrost overnight.

## LIME AND COCONUT CAKE

This beautiful fresh cake combines tart limes with creamy coconut. It is delicious at any time of the year, but its fresh, lively flavors make it ideal for a summer wedding. The addition of creamed coconut means that this cake is best baked in 2 halves, then sandwiched together.

**ingredients for 6-inch round cake**

⅔ cup (1⅓ sticks) unsalted butter, softened

¾ cup golden superfine sugar

1⅓ cups self-rising flour, sifted

3 large eggs, beaten

1 tbsp. milk

⅓ (7-oz.) block creamed coconut, grated

**bake:  convection 340°F**
**conventional 375°F**

**1** Preheat the oven. Have all the ingredients at room temperature. Grease and line 2 deep cake pans with nonstick baking paper. Put all the cake ingredients into a large bowl and whisk together until you have a smooth batter.

**2** Divide the batter betweeen the 2 prepared pans and smooth the surface. Bake in the oven 20 minutes (plus or minus 15 minutes per 2 inches of pan size) until risen, light golden, and the cakes spring back when pressed. Let cool a little, then remove the cakes from the pans and place on a wire rack to cool completely. Sandwich with lime and coconut buttercream (see page 137).

**TO STORE**  Store in an airtight container and eat within 2 days. This cake is not suitable for freezing.

# TEMPLATES

### PETITE ROSE
See page 61

### WINTER SNOWFLAKES
See page 109

### TREE OF LIFE
See page 86

**LACE VEIL**
See page 54

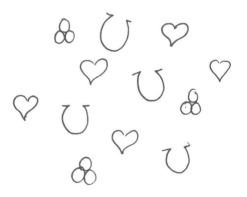

**COUTURE CONFETTI**
See page 67

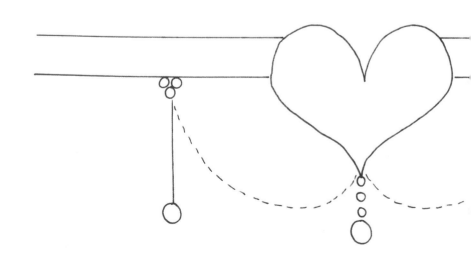

**QUEEN ELIZABETH DIAMOND: 12 IN.**
See page 22

**VENETIAN**
See page 29

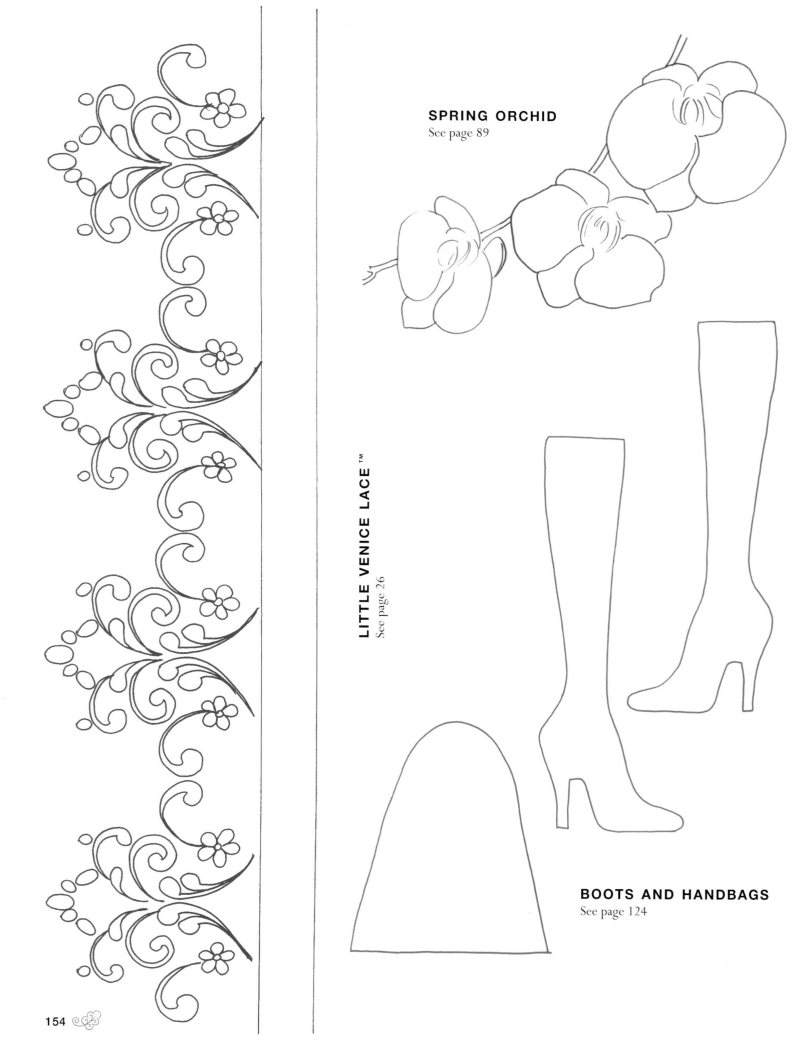

**SPRING ORCHID**
See page 89

LITTLE VENICE LACE ™
See page 26

**BOOTS AND HANDBAGS**
See page 124

**ANTIQUE ROSE**
See page 48

**CORSETIÈRE**
See page 37

**GOLD-PAINTED ROSES**
See page 116

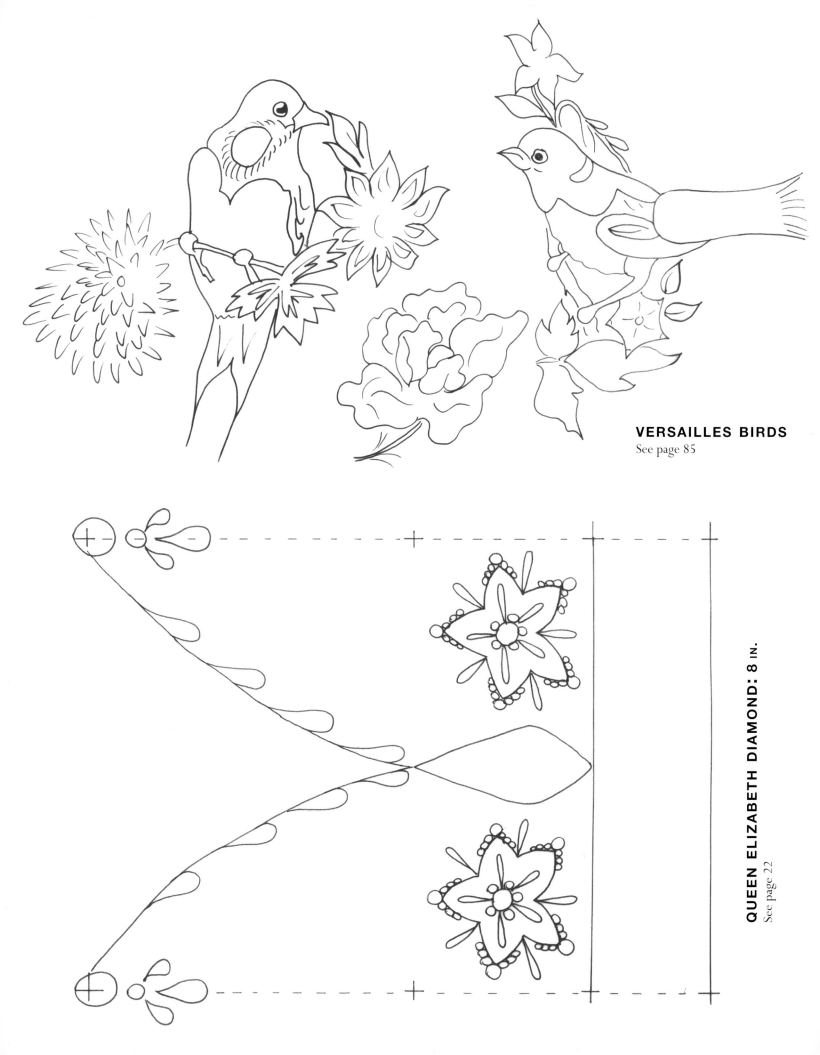

**VERSAILLES BIRDS**
See page 85

**QUEEN ELIZABETH DIAMOND: 8 IN.**
See page 22

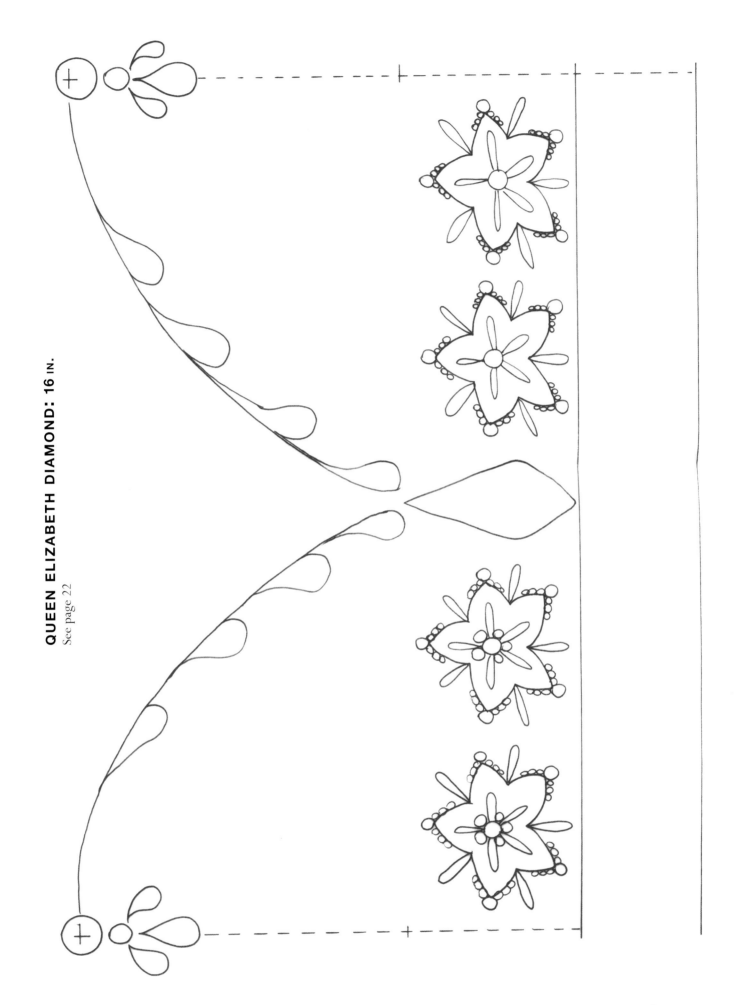

**QUEEN ELIZABETH DIAMOND: 16 IN.**
See page 22

# MARKING PILLARS ON A CAKE

See pages 142 and 143

For round and square cakes up to 10 inches, use 4 pillars positioned at **A** or **B**. For larger cakes use 8 pillars, positioned at **A** and **B**.

For hexagonal-shaped tiers use either 3 or 6 pillars, positioned at **C**, **D** or a combination of both.

10 in. cake

9 in. cake

8 in. cake

14 in.

12 in.

10 in.

8 in.

Follow C for 3 pillars,
C + D for 6 pillars

14 in.
12 in.
10 in.
8 in.
14 in.
12 in.
10 in.
8 in.

**B**
**C**

14 in.
12 in.
10 in.
8 in.
14 in.
12 in.
10 in.
8 in.

**B**
**C**

A/D

14 in. 12 in. 10 in. 8 in.

**A**

**A**

8 in. 10 in. 12 in. 14 in.

Follow A or B for 4 pillars,
A + B for 8 pillars

**D**

8 in.
10 in.
12 in.
14 in.

8 in.
10 in.
12 in.
14 in.

**B**

**D**

8 in.
10 in.
8 in.
10 in.
12 in.
14 in.

**B**

A/C

8 in.

10 in.

12 in.

14 in.

# USEFUL ADDRESSES

**Beryl's Cake Decorating & Pastry Supplies**
P.O. Box 1584
North Springfield, VA 22151
Phone: 800-488-2749 / 703-256-6951
Fax: 703-750-3779
www.beryls.com

**Broadway Panhandler**
65 East 8th Street
New York, NY 10003
Phone: 212-966-3434 / 866-COOKWARE (266-5972)
Fax: 212-966-9017
www.broadwaypanhandler.com

**Kitchen Crafts**
P.O. Box 442
Waukon, IA 52172-0442
Phone: 800-298-5389 / 563-535-8000
Fax: 800-850-3093 / 563-535-8001
www.kitchenkrafts.com

**New York Cake & Baking**
56 West 22nd Street
New York, NY 10010
Phone: 800-942-2539 / 212-675-2253
Fax: 212-675-7099
www.nycake.com

**Pastry Chef Central, Inc.**
1355 West Palmetto Park Road, Suite 302
Boca Raton, FL 33486-3303
Phone: 888-750-CHEF (2433) / 561-999-9483
Fax: 561-999-1282
www.pastrychef.com

**Pattycakes, Inc.**
34-55 Junction Boulevard
Jackson Heights, NY 11372-3828
Phone: 866-999-8400 / 718-651-5770
www.pattycakes.com

**Sugarcraft**
2715 Dixie Highway
Hamilton, OH 45015
Phone: 513-896-7089
www.sugarcraft.com

**Sweet Celebrations, Inc.**
(formerly Maid of Scandinavia)
P.O. Box 39426
Edina, MN 55439-0426
Phone: 800-328-6722 / 952-943-1508
www.sweetc.com

**The Ultimate Baker**
4917 East 2nd Street
Spokane Valley, WA 99212
Phone: 866-285-COOK (2665) / 509-954-5753
Fax: 225-410-9048
www.cooksdream.com

**Wilton Industries**
2240 West 75th Street
Woodridge, IL 60517
Phone: 800-794-5866 / 630-963-1818
Fax: 888-824-9520 / 630-963-7196
www.wilton.com

# ACKNOWLEDGMENTS

It is not surprising that I have discovered a passion for designing couture wedding cakes—my mother studied fashion design at art college and my father's ancestors were master enamellers on the canal boats. As such it has been a pleasure and an indulgence to present a collection of cake designs in this book—with the following thanks:

To my publishing team: Jacqui Small for the opportunity: Lesley for the best initiation you could have; Richard for your stunning photography (with so many girls in your life you have certainly captured the essence of each and every cake); Alison for being so persistent and pedantic with your editing; the fabulous Maggie and Bev for your unfaltering support, hard work, and commitment; also a special thank you to Sarah Cuttle and Janine Hosegood for the extra shots.

To my fabulous team at Little Venice Cake Company: Christine (Boo) Lee, who assisted with so many of the hand-decorated iced designs; Colin Chih—you so OWN chocolate; and Camilla Casey and Caroline Morgan for making it all run so smoothly. I am proud of you all and enjoy working with such a talented, passionate team.

To the amazing team at Limelight Management—Fiona, Mary, Alison, and Leonie.

To the lovely Esther at Chanel, Old Bond Street.

To Paul Reader and Charlotte Holt at Boodles—thank you for boodling me!

It has been an enormous challenge to photograph each and every one of these cakes on location—my immense thanks to the following individuals who generously gave their venues, flowers, props, and time to assist with bringing these cakes to life:

STUNNING VENUES—Thomas Kochs (Liebchen) and Mark Tucker at The Connaught; Carl Chapman at Claridge's; Gordon Ramsay and Michelle Chillingworth at Gordon Ramsay's Amaryllis Room at Claridge's; the gorgeous Gareth Bush at The Dorchester; everyone at Beach Blanket Babylon and The Soho Hotel; Rachel Hill at Lucknam Park; Thierry Lepinoy at Whatley Manor; Justin Odell at The Hempel; Chris Thompson at The Landmark; Amanda Mellett at RSA and Sinead Flynn at 30 Pavilion Road

FABULOUSLY TALENTED FLORISTS—Neil Birks, Paul Thomas, Mark at TUFF, Jill Jeffries, Sue Barnes at Lavender Green, Jamie Aston, Mary Jane Vaughan, and Helen at Jane Packer flowers

PASSIONATE AND PROFESSIONAL WEDDING / EVENT PLANNERS—Kathryn Lloyd, Amanda Sherlock, and Germaine Giles (Giles Sherlock Event Design), and Sarah Haywood

PERFECT PROPS—Thomas Goode, Jones Hire, Great Hire, Osborne and Little, General Trading Company, Lea Doherty, Asprey, Andrew Prince Jewellery

Thank you to all the fashion designers who constantly design and therefore inspire me—especially Amanda Wakeley for your support.

Finally, thank you to my amazing family—Phil, Marlow, and George: you make everything worthwhile.